Western Thought
for Asian Readers

Western Thought
for Asian Readers
Traditions of Greeks, Romans, Jews, and Christians

by
D.L. Johnson

Decent Books
New Delhi

Published and printed by:
Decent Books
D-36/A-1, Mohan Garden
Najafgarh Road
New Delhi - 110 059
Ph. (011) 2535-3435

Distributed by:
D.K. Printworld (P) Ltd.
Regd. office : *'Sri Kunj,'* F-52, Bali Nagar
New Delhi - 110 015
Phones : (011) 2545-3975, 2546-6019; *Fax* : (011) 2546-5926
E-mail : dkprintworld@vsnl.net
Web : www.dkprint.com

ISBN 81-86921-25-7

First Published in India in 2004

Preface

THIS is a book for Asian readers curious about Western culture. It is a general survey of some of the major books as well as dominant ideas that have, over centuries, shaped Western culture. The survey is done in two volumes. The first carries the title *Western Thought for Asian Readers: Traditions of Greeks, Romans, Jews and Christians*. The second volume is sub-titled *Popular Culture: Books, Movies, Clothing and Cars*. The first treats the "high culture" of the Western world. The second treats the culture that is popular and appealing to many young people in the West.

This book is a consideration of those works of literature which have been of fundamental importance in shaping the culture and society in which Western people, particularly Americans, live today. It might be argued that some of the ideas, which once were an important part of Western traditions, are not highly regarded today (that is to say, some people think many of the "old ideas" to be irrelevant and unimportant).

But Asian readers, who encounter Western people, will find that, indeed, traditional ideas and values do continue as important matters — even if they are thought by some to be matters which need to be countered, even negated. For example, many Western women, today, are not happy about the way women were valued in the classical era (that is to say, valued often as property). But women's opposition to older ideas and values does imply that the ideas linger enough to be opposed. Moreover, some people are not happy with the claims of Christianity against the teachings of Hindu or Buddhist faiths.

Related, of course, is a problem which confuses many Asian people, Western thinkers (philosophical or religious) assert many of their ideas as truth claims. About this matter philosophers are, sometimes, less aggressive than religious thinkers. Jewish, Christian and Muslim thinkers assume that what they assert is true, even as they disagree with one another. In other words, religion is often a controversial matter in the West.

Traditional Indian and Chinese thinkers did not make much of truth-claims when discussing either philosophy or religion. The assumption of major Asian thinkers seems to have been that both philosophy and religion ask a person to embrace a way of living. Each promoted a culture, a value system to be adopted as a way to conduct life in an orderly society.

It might be the influence of Greek philosophy in the West that has inclined many religious thinkers to put their ideas into assertive terms. What is written or stated is to be taken as either true or false. Such an inclination is thought to be confusing, possible foolish, by Indian and Chinese thinkers who are not uncomfortably troubled by differences among religious assertions and practices. An Asian person easily assumes that celebrations of Christmas or Easter need not imply truth-claims about a virgin birth or about the resurrection of a dead man. But that is not always so for some Westerners. So, an Asian reader must be aware of the tendency of many people in the West to make religion something which it is not for an Asian person. People of the West argue about religion, about ritual, and, sometimes, even about philosophy. Such arguments might seem to be slightly "distateful" and, certainly, unnecessary for an Asian person. But, then, cultural differences need to be recognized and understood. They do not need to be endorsed.

This volume will begin with a survey of ancient Greek philosophy and conclude with a consideration of Christian religion. Particular attention will be given to the way in which early Christian thinkers adopted Greek philosophical categories as a way to make a case for what they saw to be the truth-claims of Christianity. Thus, the book begins with Greek philosophy and ends with efforts to synthesize that philosophy with the claims of the Chirstian religion.

Contents

Acknowledgements

I with to express deep appreciation to the Department of Humanities and the University Honors Program at Indiana State University. These programmes provided occasion for extended study with and presentations to students in America, China, and India. Under the direction of D.L. Jennermann, both programmes were a source of wonderful academic challenges and rewards. Additionally, there was Dr. Jennermann's administrative ability to make available for me time and money to travel to Asia again and again. And it is with gratitude that I acknowledge his generous assistance and encouragement.

2003 **D.L. Johnson**

1

The Greek Legacy

THE period of ancient Greece (often referred in the West as the Classical Age) is remarkable for what it gave to the Western culture. Many people in the East and the West are convinced that it was the Greeks who invented Democracy. The Greeks did install a democratic government, argued about it, and abandoned it. Nevertheless, although abandoned, Greek democracy remained for many people an enduring idea. For, along with the experiment with democracy, the major questions of free societies were raised and argued.

For example, it was the Greeks who raised the question: "Is it wrong (against nature, indeed) to enforce slavery?" and, "What is the ultimate source of law (is the source, human or is the source, divine)?" Are families basic to a sound social order or should families be abolished? Plato, a Greek thinker, wrote that families should be abolished and the government should be assigned the work of overseeing the development of children.

Another question, raised by the Greeks, was whether civil disobedience might, sometimes, be a proper course of action for citizens to take when it is thought that a government does not govern properly. Sophocles gave an enduring discussion of this matter in his tragic drama, *Antigone*. And, again, it was the Greeks who raised the question of what is the proper relationship of the sexes. Are men and women equal in all ways? Aristophanes ridiculed the idea that women might be competent to hold public office. But, as well, the question was raised of what justifies the authority of a government (other than the exercise of ruthless power). And, at another level, a question was raised as to what the role of heredity might be in the formation of character. And what might be the role of education in the formation of character?

And it was by the Greeks that characteristic literary forms of Western culture were invented. First was the Epic poem, which provided a narration of heroic actions by persons of high achievement. The work of Homer (*The Iliad, The Odyssey*) became the model for later writers such as Virgil, Dante, and Milton.

Other literature, to be credited to the Greeks, is poetry. *Lyric Poetry* as well as *Tragic drama* and *Comic drama* all can be traced to Greek culture. Probably, the most widely read inheritor of these literary forms in the West was William Shakespeare (1564-1616).

And yet, another form of literature is the *essay*, used by the Greeks for the writing of history and philosophy. The novel emerged from the essay form, at a later date.

The philosophical legacy is vast. There can be no understanding of philosophy as it is done in the Western world without knowing what Plato and Aristotle wrote. That is to say, that these men raised the enduring questions for philosophers of Western culture. In fact, some have argued that philosophy, since Plato and Aristotle, amounts to little more than commentaries and footnotes, related to their work. Moreover, one cannot understand the significance of the phrase from the Christian *New Testament*,

"In the beginning was the Word" without having some sense of what Greek thinkers meant by *Word* (*Logos*).

When doing philosophy, the Greek thinkers also invented what is known as *Textual Criticism*. Textual Criticism involves three areas of study: the study of history (to discover the context out of which a text emerged), the study of texts, themselves (to discover which of available texts are authentic) and the study of sources (to discover where a particular writer might have gotten the information provided in the text).

And, one might add, the modern cult of athletics and the athlete as hero began with the Greeks. The Western world, especially in recent decades, has seen athletics, turned into nothing short of religion.

The Background to the Greek Culture

There never was a nation, called Greece in the ancient world. Instead, there were people who called themselves *Hellenes* (Hel e neeze). These people shared a common language, a common (although somewhat diversified) religion and a sense of a common history.

The mainland of Greece is the Balkan peninsula which is joined to a large land mass, known as the Pelponessus by a narrow strip of land. The territory, we call Greece, was invaded from the north in the twelfth or eleventh centuries BC and many of the mainlanders fled to the Asiatic coast of the Aegean Sea and its islands. There, they organized themselves into a number of small city-states.

Later, in the seventh and sixth centuries BC, many of the city-states sent out colonists to occupy new territories. This expansion resulted in many new Greek cities all over the land mass today known as Turkey, Italy and Sicily. These small cities, though often at war with one another, shared a common language, a common group of stories about gods and goddesses and ideals of culture. They regarded all those who did not speak their language (Greek) as *barbaros* (barbarians, strangers).

The Ancient Minoan Influences

As early as 1900 BC, a group of tribes from northern Europe and begun to move slowly into the peninsular region of Greece. By 1600, they had occupied all of the mainland, including the Peloponessus and they established a city, known as Mycenae (my SEE nee). The Myceneans took control of the island of Crete. One of the kings of Mycenae was named Agamemnon, about whom one reads in Homer's, *The Odyssey*. And a major tragic drama carries the name Agamemnon.

Mycenean culture lasted from the sixteenth century until the twelfth century. These people emphasized what are today thought to be "masculine" traits of strength, courage, and personal honour. Human worth, for these people, was thought to lie in personal accomplishment, often accomplishment that might be won through warfare. Battlefield exploits could bring death, but they also bring honour, and, in time, fame. And such exploits were often the result of wily, even tricky, intelligence. Brutal strength alone did not make a hero. Odysseus in *The Odyssey* displays this ideal of a wily intelligence almost to perfection.

The Trojan War and The Iliad

Homer's epic poem *The Iliad* is set against the background of the Trojan War, the battle for the city of Troy. The city (also referred to as Ilium) was beseiged for ten years and finally sacked by the Greek king, Agamemnon, and his noble friends who had rallied to his cause. That cause was to gain the return of Helen, the beautiful wife of Menelaus, king of Sparta, who had been stolen by the Trojan prince, Paris. Important characters in the story told by Homer are Agamemnon (brother of Menelaus), Priam (king of Troy), Priam's son Paris, and Odysseus (king of Ithaca).

The armies of Agamemnon and Odysseus defeated the city of Troy by means of a trick. A huge wooden horse (the "Trojan Horse") was delivered to the king of Troy as a sign of the Greek armies' desire for peace. But the huge horse was filled with soldiers. And once inside the city, the soldiers attacked. The date often given for this clever, but deceitful, strategy of warfare is 1184 BC.

The Odyssey

The author of the epic poem *The Odyssey* is thought to be the same Homer who wrote *The Iliad*. Although Homer himself lived in the late eighth century BC, the events, he wrote about, occurred centuries earlier. *The Odyssey* is the story of the return of Odysseus from the battle of Troy. To write the story, Homer drew from various stories and legends about Odysseus and others. In fact, Homer used the actual return of Odysseus as, but a framework, to allow him to tell, once again, all sorts of stories, familiar to the people at that time.

The events narrated by Homer might have occurred as early as the twelfth century BC — a period often called the "Homeric Age." The period of time was marked by a "partriarchal society." Among the wealthy in such a society, women and slaves did most of the important work. Relationships among related families and within a family were strongly emphasized. Government was by a council of nobles (an aristocracy), usually under the leadership of a king. But, in addition to nobles and slaves, there were craftsmen, merchants, sailors, minstrels, and even physicians. According to stories told by Homer, it seems that the noble families kept themselves busy with banquets (feasting), athletic events, dancing and entertainment, provided by minstrels. Homer was, apparently, one such entertainer.

Whereas *The Iliad* deals with the tenth year of the Trojan War, *The Odyssey* begins in the tenth year *after* the fall of Troy. Odysseus, alone of the surviving Greek heroes, has failed to return home. He has had to suffer ten years of wandering because he offended the sea god, Poseidon. And all of his soldiers have died because they offended the sun god, Hyperion.

The epic is divided into 24 books. The first four books set a scene before Odysseus even enters the action. The gods of Mount Olympus have gathered to discuss the fate of Agamemnon (murdered by his wife Clytemnestra and her lover Aegisthus as soon as he returned from Troy). The story of Agamemnon provides a moral contrast between two heroes: Agamemnon's wife has been faithless; Homer's wife, we soon discover, has withstood the greedy and rude attention of many men who want her. Next, the gods discuss Odysseus and they conclude that he has suffered enough and he sould be allowed to return home.

The reader meets Odysseus in Book 5 on the island of Ogygia. The gods have just decided that Hermes, their envoy, should be despatched to release Odysseus. But, then, the goddess Athena, Odysseus' champion and protector, visits Odysseus' palace in Ithaca and works to motivate Telemachus, Odysseus' son, to do his duty as a son and to take active steps toward finding his long-lost father.

Books 5-8 tell of Odysseus' journey from Calypso's island to the land of the Phaeacians. Books 9-12 present Odysseus' adventures from the time he left Troy to the time he was stranded on Calypso's island. Books 13-24, constituted the second half of *The Odyssey.* And it might be titled *Odysseus' Revenge.* On a boat, provided by the Phaeacians, whom he befriended, Odysseus returns to Ithaca. To conceal his identity from the obnoxious suitors who are trying to convince Penelope that her husband is dead, Athena transforms Odysseus into a wrinkled old man. Odysseus spends time exploring his island, and, then, lays a plot for revenge against the men who are harrassing his wife.

Odysseus finds refuge in the hut of his faithful swineherd, *Eumaeus.* Telemachus, who was visited Sparta and Pylos to inquire about the fortunes of his father, returns home, and, under Athena's protection, goes to Eumaeus' hut, immediately. Father and son are re-united, and they plan revenge against the hundred or more suitors lounging about Odysseus' palace grounds.

Revenge, as it eventually occurs, is one of merciless slaughter. Vengeance belongs to a hero, Homer informs his readers. After the slaughter, Odysseus and Penelope are re-united. And a final reconciliation with Odysseus' father Laertes takes place. And, so, ends the epic story of a Greek hero.

2

Greek Religion in The Iliad and The Oddyssey

GREEK religion may seem peculiar to many who are associated with one of the so-called "Great Traditions" of world religions, viz., Hinduism, Buddhism, Confucianism, Taoism, Judaism, Christianity and Islam. There are, of course, differences among the Great Traditions. But the ancient Greek religion provides something completely different from any of the Great Traditions. Yet, ancient Greek religion must be classified, technically, as a Western religion.

Differences are striking. For Greek religion, there was no institutional system or organization that is known to have existed. Moreover, there seems to have been no known sense of history for the rituals and practices. In fact, there seems to have been no sense of a beginning for the religion. So far as is known, there was no prominent prophet or law-giver. And there were no sacred books whose authority was thought to be final in matters of morality and belief. And there was no central authority or hierarchy of priests or bishops. And there was no "revealed" cosmology or theory about where the earth came from and why human beings are, as they are. In short, Greek religion was very, very different from the religious traditions known to most Western people today. There was, however, a mythology, a mythology known and accepted as truth by the Greek people who are written about in *The Iliad* and *The Odyssey.* Such a mythology told of a beginning in which there was chaos, emptiness, darkness. From the chaos there emerged a god and a goddess (it is not clear how they emerged). From their union came the *Titans*, a race of gods. One of the Titans, *Kronus*, led a revolt against his father Uranus and overthrew him (from the blood of Uranus came the fearful hags known as *Furies*, whose duty it was to pursue anyone who had shed the blood of a relative). Kronus took his sister *Rhea* as his wife (Rhea in the mythology is associated with earthly forces). It is Kronus and Rhea who produced the gods of Mount Olympus.

An unfortunate complication to the whole matter, however, was that Kronus had prophecy in his background that one of his children would overthrow him; to prevent this he swallowed all of his children at birth. Rhea was unhappy with this solution to Kronus' worries and she tricked him and managed to save one child (Rhea handed him a stone wrapped in a blanket and Kronus swallowed the stone).

The saved child was Zeus, to be known as lord of the sky. Zeus led a revolt against his father, aided by some of the Titans and shut up Kronus in a cave. But, before his captivity, Kronus managed to vomit up the other children that he had swallowed: *Demeter*, *Hera* (*hear a*), *Pluto*, *Poseidon*, and *Vesta*. Zeus took Hera as his wife and they produced gods and goddesses: *Athena* (goddess of intelligence, lover of fine things), *Aphrodite* (goddess of fertility), *Artemis* (goddess of perpetual virginity and wild nature), among others.

An important feature of the gods is that they know a great deal more than humans know, and they can communicate crucial information to people at critical times. For example, at the shrine of the god Apollo at Delphi, a priestess, inspired by the god, would enter a trance and say what were thought to be important words of insight and prediction. It was thought that a god possesses extraordinary knowledge.

The gods were thought to move among people (that is, they were in some sense around people, even though people might be unaware of them). Yet, people were not expected to practice any special form of self-abasement or humility before them. And like Greek heroes, the gods were moved by a consideration of personal honour. So, people related to gods by attempting to cultivate their favour and avoid their anger. What was thought to be a god's mood or inclination at a particular time was an important consideration concerning how a person should act. Thus, there was an uncertainty about gods as well as a disinclination to accept them as appropriate models for human behaviour. Nevertheless, gods needed to be recognized and acknowledged as possessing power. But the power might be used in unpredictable ways.

That is to say, the gods were not much concerned with good or evil in a moral sense. They might interfere with people's lives (although not ordinarily on the basis of right or wrong human behaviour). Interference with human behaviour had to do with a god feeling favourably disposed or revengeful towards a person (that is to say, people might do things that could injure a god's sense of self-esteem).

In short, Greek religion appears to have been a cult of power: there need be no love or devotion to a god. Instead, barter and trade controlled relationships to gods. So, it is not necessarily the weak who get help from the gods. Someone who has struck a bargain with the gods gets help.

The After-Life

There is no single unified teaching about the after-life in ancient Greek religion. There are some differences in the texts where an after-life is discussed. The general teaching is that souls continue after the death of people and the souls bear a resemblance to the physical appearance of the body (yet, there is no substantial material surviving, there is no physical body). Conversations with the dead are possible by the proper offerings of milk, honey, wine, and water. Blood poured into a trench might bring souls of the dead to it because souls are attracted by the odour of fresh blood.

Death is not a good thing. Achilles says that he would rather be a servant in the house of some landless man than king of all the dead. Yet, the condition of the dead is not one of torment. Instead, it is a place where no heroic activity is possible. And that, to the Greeks, was a bad situation.

What is the good life to live, then? who is a good man? The Greeks took many centuries to spell this out, but two ideas are clear by the sixth century BC. As early as Homer, there seems to be no sense of a "good man" in ethical terms. A good man for Homer is someone proficient in doing something — fighting, ruling, out-witting enemies. Homer's view might seem shallow.

In later writing, four moral qualities are notable. They are *courage, temperance, justice* and *wisdom*. The list is thought to be attributable to Pythagoras. The list appears in his work and the ideal continued to be mentioned by others from the sixth to even beyond the fourth century BC.

The ideal embodies what the Greeks admired in theory and tried to put into practice: that is, if a person exercises these virtues and applies them in each situation, then he is doing as much as can be expected of him as a human being. *Courage* refers to the physical aspect of a man and for the Greeks this had much to do with war (note that all of the great writers and thinkers had been soldiers at one time in their lives; and a man was expected to be available for military service until he was sixty years old). *Temperance* refers to a manner or style, a way of doing things without display or vulgarity, of behaving without arrogance. In one sense Temperance was a matter of good manners: Pericles said, "Our love of what is beautiful does not lead us to extravagance; our love of the things of the mind does not make us soft."

Justice refers to a moral quality, the natural inclination to obey the rules and the laws of a civilized society and to give to other men what they deserve, rendering to every man his due. The word for justice is *dike* (dee kay) and means to keep within the boundaries of one's own abilities and to respect what are thought to be the boundaries of others. *Wisdom*, of course, refers to the intellectual quality of a man's life: it denoted, for the Greeks, a skill in the arts as well as a capacity for philosophy and politics.

These ideals are extended when applied to the social life required for city-states that were established. *Courage* could be prized both for its own sake and for its use to the city (physical bravery is not enough; a person must be able to fight for a cause that is shared with others). *Temperance* came to mean that a person ought to know one's limitations and to curb ambition and pride (to "know thyself," in Socrates' words). Personal ambitions must, sometimes, be curbed and restrained for the good of society.

Justice, as a social virtue, came to mean not just personal relations with others but effort to establish a just society (questions got raised about what might be required to build a perfect society). *Wisdom* came to mean a person's ability to think carefully in order to do just the right thing at the right time, to have foresight as to the consequences which might occur from doing a specific act.

The good life has another sense apart from moral goodness. For the good life there must be wealth, physical beauty, health, happiness (which often meant good times in the company of friends). These matters have not so much to do with what a person does but with what a person has and is. Yet the Greek thinkers seemed to believe that if one is not first a good man, it is unlikely that he could enjoy the good things of life.

Some emphasis is put upon good health. To be unhealthy is to be in a sense out of control, to be at the mercy of sickness and disease. In fact, what might be called a "cult of the body" arose among the Greeks. It seems that belief in health passed quickly to belief in the beauty of the human body. The Olympic games, of course, emerged from this interest in physical beauty as well as the idea that such beauty could come from physical fitness and "physical development." To be a winner in the games was thought to be the realization of good health: and if a winner, a man deserved honour for achieving the best in skill and strength.

As for the pursuit of wealth, it was not to be an end in itself Wealth was simply a means by which a man could live the good life. The Greeks saw no good in poverty and the suffering and debasement that comes with it (note that this differs from another tradition of thought in the West that implies that a vow of poverty is good). But for the Greeks, a man who loses his money soon loses his friends.

Yet a fourth good is to be young and be among friends.

There was much encouragement to extend youthfulness and, in a sense, to ignore ageing. Socrates went to war when he was 47 years old; all Greeks were expected to serve in the army if there was a war until the age of 60. Emphasis upon athletics and good health seemed to have consequences: Gorgias died when he was older than 100 years; Zenophanes died at 92; Democritus lived past 90; Sophocles died, aged 90; and Plato died at 82. All of this is to say that the Greeks seemed to have little or no notion of an ascetic or puritanical hostility to pleasure. But temperance was to rule here as well. The good life must be kept in its place and within its proper boundaries.

3

The Odyssey as Epic Literature

Basic Elements of Literature

THE basic elements of traditional Western literature are four: plot, character, setting and theme. Plot refers to the action. What happens in a story. Usually, action occurs as a situation which requires a solution. The situation might be any sort of human issue, including conflicts, misunderstandings or adventures. The action, therefore, involves complications which might bring about tension, anxiety and frustration. The series of incidents, which bring about a resolution of the complications, constitute the plot of a story. In some works of literature, there might be two or more plots running, side by side. But, usually, one plot is regarded as the major plot and others as minor plots. The major plot works to resolve the major complication.

The Odyssey has three plots, which the author cleverly integrates into one plot. The major plot is the story of Odysseus' effort to return to his home at Ithaca. There are many complications to this plot — the Lotus Eaters, the Cyclops, Circe, Scylla and Charybdis, not to mention beautiful and seductive Calypso. The second plot, actually introduced first to the reader, is the story of Odysseus' son, Telemachus, and his difficult growth to manhood. The third plot is Odysseus' actual return and his revenge against the men, who have been harrassing his wife and household.

A second element of literature has to do with *Character(s)*. Plot and character are integrated carefully in a good story. Characters relate to or carry on the events of the plot. But characters must also be something or someone in and by themselves, apart from the plot. The critical question, which lurks in the background for a reader, is the question of how *believable* a character might be. That is, does a character, as a person, *fit* with the action of the plot? Or, might a character, as a person, be someone unlikely to fit with the action of the plot? For example, would it be believable to have a weak character, suddenly, doing heroic things?

Another element of literature, requiring the attention of a reader, is the "setting." The time and the place, where action occurs, is the "setting" of a story. Because time and place are specific, the customs, beliefs and values, known to be true of a place and time, must be consistent with the plot and characters. It would not do to have Odysseus smoking a hookah or riding an elephant, since hookahs and elephants were not a part of the "setting" in which Odysseus would be found.

Another matter, about which thought must be given in literature, is the element of *Theme*. Not the same as Plot, "Theme" has to do with the point of view that the writer conveys. What is the writer attempting to tell his readers by telling them about these events and these characters? A critical reader needs to ask, "What is the author's understanding of human life, which he is revealing by telling us about these events and these characters?"

And finally, related to "Theme," is the matter of *Narrator*. Who is telling the story? Generally, there are three types of Narrators: an Omniscient Narrator (one who knows everything that can be known about what is taking place); a Character Narrator (someone in the story, itself, who tells it in the first person — "I went there, I saw this, I did that"); and the Limited Narrator (the author knows enough to tell the story, but the author does not know everything).

Ways of Telling a Story

There are five different ways to tell a story. One might start at the beginning and go through to the end. Or, one might tell the story through the eyes of different people, different characters in the story. Or, one might tell it from a point sometime after the events have taken place. These three ways are fairly conventional and they are the ways in which most stories are told.

A fourth, and more complicated way of telling a story, is to tell the story without any regular sequence of events. This way forces the reader to put the story together as he reads it (or hears it). The "stream of consciousness" technique used by some contemporary writers employs this way of telling a story. Finally, one might tell a story by beginning very near the end. This is the method that is employed by Homer in *The Odyssey*.

The Artistic Structure of The Odyssey

Little is known about the poet, Homer. From the specific style of Greek language, used in *The Odyssey* and *The Iliad*, it is assumed that Homer lived in the eighth or ninth century BC. No biographical or autobiographical literature exists which might be trusted to give a fair account of the man.

There has been some scholarly speculation that the same man did not write both *The Odyssey* and *The Iliad*. Some have argued that the works are products of groups of anonymous bards, to whom the name, Homer, was, later, applied as something of a collective term. But, contemporary scholarship, in general, holds that each of the poems has a consistency of style and outlook that shows them to be the work of one writer.

The Odyssey is the product of a period in which, what we know as literature was a tale told by a story-teller. *The Odyssey* was not written as a book until a much later time than the events that are told. It is thought that Homer was a professional bard (a person who lived by composing, reciting, and telling to people the legends and mythologies of the Greek tribes). The oral origins of the written work, we have, determines some characteristics of Greek epic literature. Five elements are clear.

An obvious characteristic of an oral origin to the story is the occurrence of *Repetition*. Phrases, lines and even groups of lines are repeated, again and again. When telling of the dawning of a new day, the lines, "And when rosey-fingered dawn appears, the child of morn" occurs over and over. The goddess Athena is referred to nearly always as "owl-eyed." The island of Ithaca is "sea-girt." And Odysseus is always "god-like."

Repetition, probably, was a device used to assist the memory of wandering story-tellers. Readers, of course, sometimes are tempted to conclude that repetition is a sign of a limited imagination. But such is not the case. The bard was composing directly before his audience (he did not memorize lines and then recite them). And to appreciate the genius of Homer it is important to note that he was dealing with a hopelessly contradictory mythology including tales of heroes, scenes of combat, descriptions of palaces, meadows, treasures, oceans and storms. And repetition of these accounts served as formulaic devices to help the poet remember. But repetition might be necessary for an audience, too. For a listener to follow along and understand a complicated story being told over many days and nights, repetition would be not only helpful but necessary.

Another characteristic of the oral epic is *Formal Rhetoric*. A great part of *The Odyssey* is made up of long, formal speeches by characters. There are many situations when the language becomes even stately. And such formal language stands in contrast to fanciful stories about unbelievable, even magical, happenings. The stately formal style probably was an aid to the poet; but it also contributes to a reader's sense of what might constitute a noble person, at that time.

Yet, another characteristic of an epic is the use of *Epithets*. An epithet is word or short phrase regularly applied to some person or thing. When applied to a person in the story, the epithet is meant to suggest a quality of character. Epithets are also an aid to both the poet and the audience. They help the reciter compose and keep essential material in mind. And they, often, afford pleasure of humour to the audience. Book IX provides a number of examples of epithets, such as "nimble-witted Odysseus," "god-like Alcinous," and "much-enduring Odysseus."

Frequent *Digressions* are also characteristic of epic literature. Sometimes, these are in the form of flashbacks to fill in necessary detail or to add a new twist to the theme (the story Odysseus tells of his journey and adventures until he reaches Calypso is actually a Digression; so also is the account of Menelaus' adventures in Book IV).

Sometimes, the Digressions contribute nothing, directly,

to the major or minor plot (for example, Odysseus' story about himself when trying to preserve his disguise; also the stories about their pasts by various minor characters, such as Eumaeus; or the little story about how Odysseus got his scar). Digressions, often, function as a "retarding element," that is, a slowing down of the action to relieve tension.

Finally, there is a *Recognition* Scene. The theme of the major plot is a movement from ignorance to knowledge. The most dramatic moments in the story involve the discovery that Odysseus has returned to Ithaca. And for some that discovery is combined with revenge. For discovery and revenge to take place, Odysseus must return in disguise. And because the discovery occurs at the time of revenge, recognition is dramatic and satisfying to the reader. Revenge and Recognition in *The Odyssey* combine to show Homer at a high artistic level.

The Odyssey's Three Plots

Homer's artistry is also shown by his skillful manipulation of three distinct plots. It is important to keep in mind that all of the material that makes up the story as we have it, was familiar to the listeners of Homer. So, Homer could not rely upon many of the story-telling devices common to listeners or readers, today. Homer was dealing with familar material. And because the material was familiar, Homer had to make his interpretation of the old stories distinct. Here again, Homer's achievement is masterful.

Homer did his work by leaving out many details which might be necessary for us to know, but for which his hearers or readers knew well. Such details would have to do with information about the Trojan War, about the intrigues concerning Agamemnon and his wife Clytemnestra (why she was mad at him, why she might want revenge). Omission of material, therefore, is the first mark of Homer's art.

A second indication of Homer's art is that he did not begin at the beginning of the Odysseus legend. Instead, he began somewhere else, almost at the end of the story. And this left him with three major plots which are clear. One plot has to do with *The Wanderings of Odysseus*. This plot consists mainly of what were probably folk stories familiar in one form or another to all. The Cyclops, the journey to Hades, the Sirens, the encounter with Scylla and Charibdas were stories, no doubt, familiar to everyone at the time. The literary question of importance is why did Homer include this material? What was the point of including all of these?

A second plot is *The Quest of Telemachus*. This is the story of Odyseeus' son Telemachus and his eventual acceptance of adult responsibility. In this case, it was the gaining of courage necessary to confront the suitors who had invaded Odysseus' home in hopes of convincing his mother to marry one of them. This plot appears immediately in the first four chapters and re-appears in later sections as well. This plot is a story in itself which carries an important theme of how a young man is to grow to accept adult reponsibilities. Again, the question to ask is why Homer wanted to make much of this theme of Telemachus' maturation.

The third plot is *The Return of Odysseus*. This is the longest section and is the second half of the epic. It follows the account of Odysseus' wanderings. And the events show him to be heroic. But the revenge scene makes good sense only in terms of the story of Telemachus and his growth to adulthood. If we did not know of Telemachus, the revenge of Odysseus would not be as satisfying to hearers and readers.

Homer tied these three plots, together. The stories are very different. One has to do with adventure, skill, cunning, heroic behaviour, etc. Another has to do with a young man growing to adulthood. The third deals almost exclusively with revenge. Odysseus pays back those who have insulted him, his wife, his son and his household.

Homer pulled together the three plots by starting with the Telemachus story, then, moving to the wandering of Odysseus story and concluding with the return and revenge story. Homer began near the end of the story, known to his hearers. To tie together the three plots, Homer made frequent references to the homecoming of Agamemnon, a story marked by Agamemnon's discovery of his wife's unfaithfulness and, then, his murder. Allusions to Agamemnon's fate occur at the very beginning with the Council of the Gods, and, again, with the discussions between Nestor and Menelaus, and again, when Odysseus visits Hades (Agamemnon in Hades himself warns Odysseus about the uncertainties of homecomings).

It is clear that *The Odyssey* is a masterful work of art. And it is clear that Homer was an extraordinary literary artist.

4

Greek Drama: The Tragic and the Comic

GREEK drama story-telling differs significantly from Greek epic story-telling. In the epic plot and action, a hero remains the same throughout the story. He does not change. What Odysseus does in his actions follows from who he is. It might even seem that his heroic actions are habitual. But a tragic hero does change. It is the nature of the tragic plot that a hero, such as Agamemnon, changes. In the tragedy, *The Agamemnon*, the great warrior, changes from being the proud man, who has taken vengeance upon Troy, into a victim of a woman's anger and unfaithfulness.

Action differs, too. The epic hero performs the significant actions of the story. The tragic hero, on the other hand, has action performed upon him. Oedipus, for example, does important things (things, he thinks important). He searches for the person responsible for his troubles. But, suddenly, the really important action, a discovery, happens to him.

The epic plot is composed of a series of episodes, which, in the end, *complete* the character (Odysseus is complete as a hero by the end of the story because he has solved all of his problems successfully). The epic actions are linked by the theme that the hero's survival is challenged by danger, and he shows himself to be heroic by doing what he must do to survive. The tragic hero, however, is destroyed by doing what he must do; and doing what he must do makes him a participant in his own destruction. Oedipus must search for the cause of his troubles. But the search destroys him.

The epic hero is responsible only for the performance of particular exploits. But he is not responsible for the existence of the problems that he solves by his heroic actions. For the tragic hero the problems are *his* problems. That is, the tragic hero is faced with problems which he himself created.

The epic hero cannot be passionate about anything; or, we might say, his passions are weaker than his habitual actions of heroism. The tragic hero is the reverse: his passions override his good deeds, whatever they might have been.

The epic poet writes about a complete heroic person. We might say that epic literature is very physical in the sense that a reader gets to know a lot about the heroic figure. Odysseus warms himself by a fire, he eats, he drinks. But the tragic poet avoids writing about anything which would attract attention to the physical part of the main character. That is, we do not see the tragic hero eating or drinking or warming himself by a fire. The tragic poet avoids ordinary physical actions because it is the moral side of a person that is the tragic poet's concern. If physical matters are allowed to enter a scene, then, comedy might enter with them.

General Characteristics of Greek Drama

There is very little action on the stage in Greek drama. Dialogue informs the audience about what has taken place off-stage. And dialogue gives information about actions that occurred before the time of the present action as well as action presently occurring off-stage. And, in spite of the fact that many of the tragic dramas are about murder, no one is ever murdered on stage.

There are no special effects such as lighting; and there is a minimum of scenery. The *impact* of the drama is meant to be intellectual and emotional. None of it is spectacular to see. Action and dialogue are directed at the minds of the audience.

The theme of Greek drama is human suffering (tragedy). It is the spiritual lives of people rather than their political or social lives that concern the writers. Characters are seen to gain stature by their inner life and inner development. There is always a change in a person's inner life in Greek drama. But Homer had little interest in such matters. Odysseus remains the same man from the beginning to the end of *The Odyssey*.

Great moral questions are raised in Greek tragedy. Is a person free to do what is right? Or are a person's actions determined by forces outside of his or her control? What is the price of war? Can the social and political costs of war ever be paid? What price is there to a person's honour? What might it cost a person to be honourable?

In tragic drama, characters are always seen taking the consequences of their own actions. No one can wipe clean the slate of his or her past actions. There is no forgiveness. Human beings are assumed to be free, but their lives are driven and determined by the acts that they do.

Greek tragedy had a chorus of onlookers who often interjected their own comments about the drama. The chorus reacts to the actions and, sometimes, to takes sides. The chorus can change sides quickly if they become convinced by speeches of the characters. The chorus plays a different role in comedy. In comedy, the chorus participates in the actions on the stage.

Minimal Characteristics of Tragedy

Tragedy involves conflict which is of universal significance. This is to say that what happens could happen to any person. The Greek philosopher Aristotle, probably, the major authority about Greek tragedy, said this: "It is an imitation of an action that is serious, complete, and of a certain magnitude; in the form of action it is not a narrative; and through fear and pity it affects the proper purgation of the emotions."

The elements of tragedy, therefore, are these: it is a serious and complete human action; it is an elevated action (that is, action done by an important person); it is a dramatic presentation (not simple story-telling); and the audience reaction is important.

Aristotle's major concern was with the form of the drama. The plot must take a certain form, he maintained. It must be *complex*. It must be an imitation of some important aspect of human life. It must deal with a character or characters who have an elevated status — that is to say, the characters must be important people. The problem which, finally, is to defeat the character must originate from an error in judgement (such an error is called "the tragic flaw"). Oedipus is a good example: he is a good king, but his tragic end comes because of what he himself does (being a good king he insists upon finding out who is responsible for the troubles of the kingdom).

Another requirement for tragedy is a Reversal. That is, an action or event which is the opposite of what is expected must occur. Agamemnon, a survivor of a brutal war, is killed when he returns home. Oedipus discovers himself when looking for someone else. The reversal involves a necessary Discovery, a recognition of who or what a person is, a recognition of truth that was hidden. Agamemnon discovered the truth about his wife and her relationship with Aegisthus. Oedipus discovered who he really was.

The plot must also involve suffering or retribution of some sort. That is, justice is to prevail, people are to receive what is due to them for past mistakes or injustices.

Characteristics of Comedy

Comedy is not simply laughter in the Greek theatre. Comedy is a plotform. The form is a movement of action through misfortune (a problem) to fortune (resolution of a problem). In the drama, *Lysistrata,* there is a war. The women propose a solution. They will withhold sexual relations with their husbands until the men agree to stop the war. Will the women be able to hold to their decision to withhold sex? Or will the men endure sexual deprivation in favour of warfare?

Comedy plots for Greek writers were built around contemporary incidents and events rather than legend or myth as were tragic plots. And there was generally some didactic purpose for a writer. That is to say, comic writers were trying to make a point, to send a message to an audience. The device used for sending a message usually was humour. And humour is simply "the juxtaposition of the incongruous." In *Lysistrata,* the message seems to be that war is not as important as sex.

Greek comedy also used *Satire* (to ridicule some behaviour in order to arouse contempt for it); *Irony* (to contrast what is said and what is actually done): *Pun* (two or more meanings implied by the same word — a double entendre); and *Shock* (scatological language, references to sex-organs or references to body wastes).

Some scholars have made distinctions between Low Comedy and High Comedy. Low Comedy uses situations, actions to elicit laughter. For example, someone pulls back a chair that a person is about to use for a seat. The person clumsily falls to the floor. And the audience laughs. *High Comedy*, on the other hand, builds upon character, not action. High comedy dramatizes the growth and development of a character as he or she goes from misfortune to happiness. There need not be occasion for an audience to laugh at High Comedy. It is the plot that is important. And in terms of plot, *The Odyssey* is actually High Comedy.

5

The Agamemnon

THE tragic drama *The Agamemnon* was written by Aeschylus, who lived from, approximately, 525 until 456 BC. He is thought to have written eighty or ninety plays but the titles of only seven are known today. The Agamemnon story is a complicated one involving an elevated character who comes to an unexpected and unhappy end. The drama illustrates very well the basic elements of Aristotle's requirements for tragedy.

The story is a long one that involves deeds and events both horrifying and sickening. But it is important to remember that it was a familiar tale. One source for the story was Homer. But Homer mentioned only selected parts of the story.

The story was referred to balefully as "The House of Atreus." And its genealogy might be charted this way:

The House of Atreus

Tantalus

Atreus Pelops Thyestes

Menelaus — Agamemnon — Pleisthenes Aegisthus — Other children killed by Atreus and served as a meal to Thyestes

Hermione Orestes — Electra — Iphigenia

The story begins with a man, named Tantalus. He was said to be a descendant of Zeus and, therefore, almost a god himself. Tantalus had a son named Pelops. In order to test whether the gods were all-knowing. Tantalus killed Pelops and served his dead son to the gods in a banquet. The gods, however, discovered the deed and restored Pelops to life.

But Tantalus was condemned to a punishment from which we derive the word "tantalize." He was made to stand in water up to his neck; however, whenever he bent down to drink, the water receded. Similarly a branch with fruit was dangled before him; but whenever he reached to take some fruit, the wind carried the fruit away, out of his reach. He was "tantalized."

Among Pelops' sons were Atreus and Thyestes. The two brothers quarrelled because Thyestes seduced Atreus' wife. Atreus fought with Thyestes and drove him from the household. Thyestes then sent Pleisthenes, Atreus' son, whom Thyestes had treated as his own son, to kill Atreus.

In the struggle, however, Atreus killed Pleisthenes, not realizing he was killing his own son. When Atreus found out whom he had killed, he pretended to consent to a reconciliation with Thyestes. Thyestes was invited to Atreus' house for dinner, and Atreus served him a meal consisting of the flesh of Thyestes' children. Atreus had butchered all of Thyestes' children except one named, Aegisthus.

When Thyestes discovered what he had done, he cursed Atreus and everyone related to him. He, then, fled with his surviving son, Aegisthus. Aegisthus, eventually, murdered his uncle Atreus.

Agamemnon and Menelaus were sons of Atreus.

Agamemnon married Clytemnestra and Menelaus married Helen. Paris, the son of the king of Troy abducted (seduced? kidnapped?) Helen and took her home to Troy. Agamemnon and Menelaus, seeking revenge for the abduction of Helen, gathered their armies and set sail for Troy. In order to obtain favourable winds for the voyage, Agamemnon put to death his own daughter, Iphigenia, as a sacrifice to Artemis, goddess of the winds.

Agamemnon and Menelaus brutally destroyed the city of Troy. But on the voyage home a storm destroyed all of Agamemnon's ships except his own. Travelling with Agamemnon was his "trophy-mistress," Cassandra.

Meanwhile, back at Myceneae, Agamemnon's city, Aegisthus was eager to rule Agamemnon's territory, Argos. He had managed to seduce Clytemnestra while Agamemnon was away. When Agamemnon returned, Clytemnestra was there to welcome him, but then she killed him. Because of Agamemnon's murder, Orestes, his son, felt duty-bound to avenge the murder by killing his mother.

No doubt, the story was as gruesome to the people of ancient Greece as it might be to people today. For generation after generation the family feud was renewed. Parents and children, brothers and sisters, husbands and wives either murdered one another or conspired to do some terrible act of revenge. And there seemed to be no way to end the cycle of brutality. The curse lay precisely in the inability of these people, given who they were, to resolve this terrible conflict.

Homer and the House of Atreus Story

Homer had his own interpretation of the House of Atreus story. For Homer, Agamemnon was a man who had been treated badly by Clytemnestra and her lover. Orestes was a model son, so far as Homer was concerned. Aegisthus, on the other hand, was an evil man who acted dishonourably by seducing a heroic leader's wife.

The bloody sacrifice of Iphigenia was not mentioned by Homer. Atreus' appalling crimes against Aegisthus and his father Thyestes were not mentioned either. For Homer, Aegisthus was a conspiring villain and Clytemnestra was a weak and unfaithful wife. Moreover, to Homer, Orestes was a dutiful son.

Aeschylus and the House of Atreus Story

Aeschylus treated the legend in three tragedies, generally, referred to as *The Orestia*. The three are *Agamemnon*, *Choephoroe* and *Eumenides*. In *Choephoroe* ("Libation Bearers"), Agamemnon's son, Orestes, is urged by the god Apollo to avenge his father's murder. With the help of his sister Electra, Orestes kills his mother, Clytemnestra, and her lover Aegisthus.

In *Eumenides* ("Kindly Ones" — a cynical reference to the Furies), the gods act to lift the curse from the House of Atreus. Orestes, who has been persecuted by the Furies for killing his mother, seeks refuge in the city of Athens and throws himself under the protection of the goddess Athena. To decide the fate of Orestes, Athena convenes the first court in the history of Athens with a group of citizens as jury. The Furies argue for Orestes' death. Apollo defends Orestes. The jury cannot decide. So Athena casts the deciding vote in favour of Orestes, and the curse is lifted. But the Furies are angry and require some convincing arguments from Athena. She promises the Furies a special place of honour in the hearts of the people of Athens.

The Agamemnon is about the homecoming of

Agamemnon, the commander of the great Greek army, which destroyed Troy. Aeschylus has this widely known story begin quietly with a watchman on the palace roof waiting for the sight of a beacon in the dark which will tell him that Troy has fallen. Suddenly, the watchman sees the beacon and runs to tell Clytemnestra. But before he goes, he hints to the audience that all is not well in Agamemnon's palace. Then the chorus enters, not yet knowing of the beacon. The chorus is made up of men, too old for military service. The chorus reminds the audience of an omen which occurred before Agamemnon's army set sail for Troy. Calchus, a seer, had said that Artemis, goddess of the winds, was hostile to Agamemnon, and that she would be appeased only by the sacrificial death of Agamemnon's daughter, Iphigenia. The chorus points out the dilemma faced by Agamemnon; join his brother in taking vengeance on Troy or save the life of his daughter. Agamemnon chose vengeance and killed his daughter.

The chorus uses violent language in condemning his choice: foul, reckless, impetuous, mad. Reference is made to "the harness of dire compulsion" when referring to Agamemnon's prideful decision. The suggestion is that, given who he was, he did not really have a choice. His sense of duty, of military responsibility, of loyalty, made the decision inevitable. The chorus does not say that Agamemnon was free to choose one way or the other. It seems to imply that life is like that. People don't really know what the consequences of an action might be. And Aeschylus has Agamemnon say, "Drop by drop in sleep falls the inevitable memory of pain: against one's will comes wisdom."

Agamemnon made some bad choices. Philosophers tend to pose questions of choice as a problem of "freedom or determinism." Either, people are free to choose or they are determined by forces within or without to do what they do. And if people are not free in their choices (if "determinism" is the case), then they cannot be held responsible for what they do. The Chorus sees the situation as more complicated than a philosopher might see it. Aeschylus suggests that all sorts of factors determine a choice. And a person cannot know for sure, in advance, what a decision might entail. Often, a person knows what needs to be known only when it is too late.

6

Sophocles and Oedipus Rex

SOPHOCLES was born around 495 and, lived pobably, until 406 BC. He was an older contemporary of Socrates. But he would have been 67 years old, when Plato was born in 428 BC. His life coincided with the rise to prominence of the city of Athens. But he also saw the demise of Athens as a military power. In short, he lived through the golden age of Athens. And he was, indeed, one who gave the age some of its glory.

Sophocles is thought to have written as many as 120 plays. Only seven of them are known to us. *Oedipus Rex* is the longest of the known Sophoclean tragedies, although it is not even half as long as Shakespeare's *Hamlet* or *Othello*. It is in the brevity of *Oedipus Rex* that we find the artistic brilliance of Sophocles. It is "tightly" written. There are no superfluous words. Every speech contributes to the rush toward the unhappy climax.

The Oedipus Story

Although the story of Oedipus was familiar to his audience, Sophocles made it a dramatic tragedy by deftly arranging events. The familiar story told of a man named Laius, king of Thebes, and his wife Jocasta, who were warned by the oracle of Apollo at Delphi that their new-born son was destined one day to kill his father and to marry his mother. Laius and Jocasta were naturally horrified by this prophecy and decided to let the child die of exposure by abandoning him in the mountains. Laius pierced the baby's feet in such a way as to prevent him from even crawling. But a shepherd found the baby, took pity on him and he gave the baby to his friend, a sheep-herder from Corinth. The man from Corinth was a servant of Polybus, King of Corinth. Since Polybus and his wife Merope were childless, they adopted the baby and named him Oedipus (swollen foot). They raised him as their own son, prince of Corinth.

Oedipus began to hear vague rumours that Polybus was not his real father. Troubled by such stories, he went to Delphi to learn the truth from the Oracle. But the Oracle repeated the original prophecy: Oedipus would murder his father and marry his mother. Thinking that Polybus and Merope were his parents, Oedipus decided not to return to Corinth while they were still alive.

Oedipus travelled through Greece and arrived eventually in the vicinity of Thebes, which, at that time, was being ravaged by a savage monster, the Sphinx. At a crossroad Oedipus encountered an old man in a chariot, escorted by several attendants. The old man was Laius on his way to Delphi to find out how to rid Thebes of the monster.

Laius and Oedipus were both hot-tempered. An argument took place about who had the right-of-way. Laius insulted Oedipus and struck him; Oedipus retaliated by killing Laius and his servants, except for one servant who escaped.

Oedipus continued on his way to Thebes, not knowing the names of any of his victims. Outside the city of Thebes, Oedipus met the Sphinx, answered her mysterious riddle, and killed her. The people of Thebes acclaimed him as a hero. And when they learned that Laius was dead, they made Oedipus their new king. He married Laius' wife Jocasta, and, in time, had four children by her, two boys (Eteocles and Polynices) and two girls (Ismene and Antigone). The prophecy was fulfilled. Oedipus had killed his father and married his mother.

Oedipus ruled wisely and Thebes prospered. But a terrible plague descended upon the city. Oedipus sent to Delphi for advice from the oracle and learned that the plague was Apollo's punishment to the city for having allowed the murder of Laius to go unpunished. Oedipus resolved to find the guilty person. His investigation, of course, led him to discover who he really was. Oedipus realized that he had committed abominable crimes by killing his father and marrying his mother. Overcome with shame and horror, he blinded himself by piercing his eyes and gave up his kingship. Jocasta, his mother/wife hanged herself. Oedipus wandered as a blind man. No one would accept him. Finally, Theseus, king of Athens, granted him sanctuary. Oedipus died peacefully at Colonus, near Athens.

Sophocles and the Oedipus Story

Sophocles, for dramatic purposes, compresses the story into just one scene. The scene is the event of Oedipus making the terrifying discovery of who he really is. But in order to compress such a story to just one scene, Sophocles had to inform his audience of events that took place before the time of the discovery (events which could not be presented on the stage), events that take place on the stage in present time, and events taking place in the present but not shown to the audience.

Events that happened before the present were, of course, the marriage of Laius and Jocasta and the birth of Oedipus. And there was the marriage of Oedipus to Jocasta. But there are also speeches in which the audience and actors are informed of Polybus' death, that Jocasta had a child raised in Corinth by others, and that Oedipus had been told that Polybus and Merope were not his real parents. These events Sophocles deals with by having actors tell of them.

Events that take place directly on the stage include the telling of past events, conversations Oedipus has with Teiresias, the blind soothsayer, and with Creon, his brother-in-law. The telling of past events let us know who Oedipus is. The occurrence of present events (dialogue with Teiresias and Creon) reveals what sort of a person Oedipus is. Dialogue indicates that Oedipus is, basically, a decent man (he has genuine pity for the city of Thebes and its troubles). But he also shows hatred for the rantings of Teiresias and scorn for Creon.

Events that take place off the stage but in the present are Jocasta's suicide and Oedipus' self-mutilation. Events over twenty years' time and many locations are compressed into one short drama lasting two hours or less. Sophocles did it by focusing rigorously upon one thing, the discovery by Oedipus of who he is. All other events have a bearing only on that one thing. In short, Sophocles compresses a whole life into one single scene.

But the self-discovery involves more than Oedipus finding out who his parents were. It involves showing him and the audience what sort of a person he is. Oedipus had a good opinion of himself at the beginning of the play. And he is proud of his accomplishment of solving the riddle of the sphinx and saving the city from destruction. Apparently, the riddle was this: what is four-footed in the morning, two-footed in the afternoon, and three-footed in the evening? The answer was man. As a baby man crawls using four limbs; as an adult man walks, using two limbs; as an old man he uses a cane as a third leg to support his weakening body.

The Complexity of Action

The drama is a detective story of sorts, but the detection is self-discovery. So, it is about a man who, with the best of intentions, destroys himself by relentlessly pursuing answers to his questions. Sophocles dramatizes the tragic content by giving us two plots that, suddenly, merge and become one. The obvious plot is Oedipus' search to find the person responsible for the present troubles. And he makes the discovery that the reason for the trouble is the murder of the king.

But there is a second plot. And that plot is the oracle's statement about killing his father and marrying his mother. This plot is hidden for a time. The *Discovery* in this tragedy is the emergence of the hidden plot to become the central issue. Oedipus exhausts the possibilities of the first plot (his search for the guilty one) when he charges Teiresias with wanting money and Creon with improper ambitions. The problem changes after his encounter with Creon. The hidden plot emerges and the awful story, foretold, comes true. There is no time interval between the discovery and the reversal: knowing the truth ruins Oedipus. Oedipus discovers that he is the one who killed Laius. He discovers that Polybus is not his father. He discovers that Laius was his father.

The *Reversal* is the destruction of the first plot (the search) and the appearance of the hidden plot. Sophocles presents a new role for a hero: the hero is his own enemy. And this is a worrisome assertion. *The Agamemnon* worked in much the same way. A first plot is Agamemnon's return as a conquering hero. Clytemnestra's revenge is the hidden plot.

There is a dramatic irony to *Oedipus Rex*. In saving himself Oedipus destroys himself. Teiresias is blind, but he is the only one who really sees. Oedipus investigates, but he is ignorant of the most important issues. When he finally does see the truth, he blinds himself. Jocasta assures Oedipus that the prophecy about him is false. But the prophecy is the proof that is needed for Oedipus to discover who he is. The act by the shepherd to save the child is actually an act of cruelty because of what will eventually happen.

And so, once again, the dramatist points out that a person cannot know the implications or consequences of what he or she might do. Does the dramatist suggest that life is far more complicated than philosophers might suspect?

7

Greek Comedy

COMEDY is a literary form. And as a literary form it does not require laughter or even efforts to get an audience to laugh. Sometimes, however, incidents and dialogue are funny. But as a plot form comedy is simply the narration of events through bad fortune to good fortune. And that does not require laughter. *The Odyssey* would be classified, technically, as "comedy." And Homer was surely not attempting to produce laughter.

The "comic plot" in Greek drama was almost always built around contemporary incidents or events. That is, reference to the present was made by means of the plot. And this makes comedy different from a literary work such as a tragedy that was built on legend or myth.

There is a *didactic* purpose to comedy. The point of it is to teach some lesson. In many cases, the device for teaching is humour. So, some comedy does elicit laughter. And there are many types of humour. One type is *satire*. This is to ridicule some form of behaviour or some character. Another type is *irony*, usually, to contrast what is said with what is done. A *pun* on the other hand, is to imply or insinuate two or more meanings to a word (for example, the Spartan "message staff" in the bawdy comedy *Lysistrada*).

Shock is another form of humour. It is usually accomplished by hyperbole in reference to sexual activities, sexual organs or even scatalogy. And finally, there is the device of solving a practical problem by means of some fantastic, unexpected, unsusual idea. In *Lysistrata,* it is the denial of sex to men as long as they seek war. It is important to remember that what is funny is strictly human. People do not laugh at a landscape. Animals are not funny except when they mimic badly some human characteristic.

Humour appeals to the intelligence. Humour requires an absence of feeling, emotion, about some matters. Intensity of feeling does not allow laughter. It is only when a person is *personally disinterested* that he or she can laugh. The appeal of the comic is to the intellect. Feelings and emotions must be set aside and the intellect made free to grasp incongruity. But it is a rare thing to laugh, alone. So, another important characteristic of humour is that it is almost always social.

A formal definition of humour is that it is the juxtaposition of the incongruous. That is, humour sets, side-by-side, two issues which, normally, are not seen together. An author might put, side by side, some sensual issue and some deeply moral issue and imply that there is a relationship between the two matters. The plot of *Lysistrata* does this: love-making and war are juxtaposed, put side-by-side; the act which might create new life is juxtaposed with killing. The two are incongruous. Yet, a moral message is presented.

Aristophanes in *Lysistrata* did not provide a serious solution to the problem of how to end warfare. He was doing something else. He was making the point that war is, in fact, counter productive. War solves no problem. Instead, war creates new problems. War is done by people who really do not understand what people need and want.

And here the comic artist calls upon people to think about what they really want. It is important to keep in mind that Aristophanes wrote *Lysistrata*, sometime near the middle of the Peloponnesian War (431-404 BC). Men were dying in battle. And Aristophanes raised the questions: is war really so important? what do we all really want?

The theme of *Lysistrata* is a serious one — the criminality of war. It is a serious theme, but Aristophanes uses humour to make his point. The plot is the effort by wives of soldiers to force them to choose peace or to be deprived of sex. The action involves specific efforts to withhold sex (even though the women find it difficult). In the opening scene, Lysistrata, a wife, convenes a conference of women representing both sides in the war. Of course, she must first convince the women of her proposal. Some of them are troubled by it.

Finally, the women agree to a two-front campaign: first, no sex; and second, to seize the Athenian acropolis which holds the treasury. The battle for the Acropolis is staged as a battle between a chorus of old women and a chorus of old men. Insults are hurled back and forth, the women pour hot water on the heads of the old men, and the women manage to chase the police away.

Lysistrata makes some insightful remarks in a debate with a police officer about whose concern a war really might be. Is it a concern for men? Or are women more affected by war? If women are most affected, they must use any weapon available to them. And Aristophanes suggests that sex is an effective weapon. And one wife, Myrrhina, who seems willing to give in to the entreaties of her deprived husband, drives her husband to frustration by her fussing about the proper place to lie down, about the mattress, the pillow, a blanket. Finally, she leaves him and urges him to vote for peace.

The resolution of the dispute is a scene where Lysistrata scolds both sides and gives reasons why they should all be friends. When the two sides begin to bicker over peace terms, she reminds the men that what they really want is sex. The bickering stops, immediately. The women prepare a banquet at the Acropolis. And all ends well.

8

Philosophy in The Classical Period

ALTHOUGH many have come to associate the city of Athens with philosophy, it is notable that, before Socrates, none of the philosophers of ancient Greece lived there. In fact, Athens was, somewhat, hostile to philosophy. Socrates was condemned to death by vote of its citizens (and the charges against him suggest that religious conservatism was stronger in Athens than in the colonies).

Athens might have remained intolerant to the point of stupidity had not the Sophists come to Athens. But, even before the arrival of Sophists, there were Greek thinkers of note, such as Pythagorus (mathematics and geometry), Parmenides (appearance and reality), Zeno (logic and paradox), and Democritus (rationality).

The Sophists were wandering scholars, some of whom called themselves *sophistai,* "teachers of wisdom." The word might be a fair equivalent to the term "professor" and, at first, had no derogatory connotation until these men ran into conflict with religion and established conservatives. Some Sophists might have deserved criticism since, as they wandered, they liked to make a living by teaching (and some charged exhorbitant fees for their instruction — Protagorus, we are told, charged ten thousand drachmas for instruction, a sum comparable to a semester's tuition at a reputable American university. And, it is true that

Sophists, prior to the fifth century BC, tended to create an attitude of scepticism, insisting, by clever means, that nothing can be known with certainty. In other words, Sophists were professional Sceptics.

Some Consequences of Scepticism

Consequences of Scepticism in Asia (China and India), generally, encouraged people toward mysticism and mystical experience (note Nagarjuna in India, Chuang tzu in China). With the Greeks, attention changed from trying to figure out what made up the universe (concerns of Pythagorus and Parmenides) to concerns about humanity (are humans distinct creatures in the world? is morality socially generated? or is morality based on reason?). That is to say, as people came to know more about other people, a suspicion that morality might be socially relative began to emerge among some thinkers. And such a conclusion is "fair game" for a sceptic.

A second consequence for Greece was that the method of study among philosophers changed. Sophists were interested in discovering and collecting *facts* about a situation rather than merely thinking about a situation. And, as well, the *purpose* of philosophizing changed with the Sophists. These men wanted to use knowledge they gained to assist in some practical matters, such as persuading or teaching.

But a change toward using knowledge to persuade raised the danger that knowledge might be used to change people's minds so that they might think differently about social and political matters. The change might be good (and, to some extent, it was good, because some Sophists were good orators who used their skills to bring a sense of cultural unity to the Greeks).

But arguments among Sophists created new problems. For example, the problem of the status of moral principles: are moral rules, standards, and ideals relative or do they apply, everywhere, and at all times? And again, the problem of knowledge: are some ideas about reality superior to others? And how do we know them to be superior?

Protagorus (ca. 490-410 BC)

Protagorus was, possibly, the most important of the Sophists. It appears that he held the respect of Socrates, and, later, Plato. He was a friend of both Pericles, the great ruler of Athens, and of Euripides, the writer of tragedy.

It is with Protagorus that the so-called subjective standpoint in doing philosophy began. What that meant was, Protagorus insisted, that our only means of certain knowledge is through our experience of sensations. His famous conclusion was that "man is the measure of all things. . . ."

Protagorus insisted that people should not look for knowledge beyond what a human being can perceive under given conditions. This simple assertion implied that all established truths and sacred principles must be subjected to analysis. But it also meant that knowledge is relative to the conditions under which knowledge is obtained.

Applying such a principle to theology, as Protagorus did, spelled trouble. In the home of Euripides he read a paper whose first sentence spelled trouble for him: "With regard to the gods, I know not whether they exist or not, or what they are like. Many things prevent our knowing: the subject is obscure, and brief is the span of our mortal life."

The Athenian Assembly responded by banishing Protagorus and ordering all people to surrender any copies of his writings to the authorities so that they might be publically burned. Protagorus fled to Sicily, but got drowned on the way.

Gorgias of Leontini

A clearer statement of Scepticism came from this man who had the good sense to stay away from Athens most of his life. Born in 483 BC, he studied philosophy and rhetoric. He went to Athens only in 427 BC as an Ambassador from Sicily.

Gorgias' teaching was that we have no knowledge of anything existing beyond the senses. If anything did exist beyond the senses, it would be unknowable, for all knowledge comes through the senses. And if anything supersensual (beyond the senses) were knowable, the knowledge of it would be incommunicable, since all communication is through the senses.

The Sophists, in spite of their Scepticism, made a significant contribution to Greek thought. They were the ones who invented grammar and logic. They developed methods of the analysis of arguments. They taught people how to detect fallacious reasoning. And it must be admitted that, after them, there came to be a demand for clarity and precision in thinking and writing. And it is to the credit of the Sophists that the ancient religion of Greece lost its hold among the intellectual classes. At the beginning of the fifth century BC, writers accepted the statements of the oracle at Delphi with piety. By 450 BC, Herodotus was criticizing the oracle. By the end of the century Thucydides openly rejected the authority of the oracle. And Euthyphro complained that, when in the Assembly, he spoke of oracles, people laughed at him as though he were an old fool. The move from docile acceptance of the old religion to outright cynicism took but a hundred years with the help of Sophists.

But many have argued that the Sophists played a major role in the deterioration of morality. Some argue that to define morality in terms of knowledge (as Protagorus did) is a credit and stimulus to thinking. But making morality a matter of reason and reflection might strike a blow at concern for character development. If morality is simply a matter of reflection, why must parents or the state give attention to nurture and character building? And the claims about the relativity of knowledge might not make people more modest, as it was probably intended to do, but instead might encourage each person to think that he/she was the measure of all things. And every clever young person could now feel himself fit to sit in judgement upon the moral code of his elders. In other words, traditional authorities and their ways were called into question by the Sophists. Yet, it must be admitted, without the Sophists, there could have been no Socrates, Plato or Aristotle.

9

Socrates and his Search for Truth

It was Socrates, who began the intellectual quest, which marks philosophy, as it was to be done in the West for 25 centuries. There are many, who have insisted, that philosophy in the West has never been much more than commentaries on the work of Plato and Aristotle. But it was Socrates who inspired both Plato and Aristotle. First, because he insisted that the philosopher's task is to find true *universal definitions*. It is not enough to settle for conventional, popular views or opinions. A genuine thinker must find what a word really means. For example, most people have in mind a meaning for the word "justice" that is derived from some particular instances of what they think to have been the occurrence of justice. Or the same with the word "courage:" a particular instance of courage produces for a person a definition of the word.

But Socrates insisted on asking, "What really is justice?" Or "What really is true courage?" Socrates believed that the task of the wise man, the man who searches for wisdom and truth, is to go beyond a particular instance of justice or of courage to find a universal definition of justice or of courage.

A second task of philosophy which Socrates advocated was the construction of Inductive Arguments. Socrates looked at various examples or instances of a thing to find what common element or characteristic might remain true of all of them. Induction is an important part of scientific investigation, particularly, investigations in the social sciences. Socrates practised induction in his search for true definitions.

Socrates is also notable because he wanted to get people to live by the standard of reason. For Socrates, knowledge is virtue (people who *know* will act morally). He insisted that no rational person knowingly does evil. To act immorally is to act contrary to reason. An example might be to tell a lie. To tell a lie is to use language to deceive someone else. But to use language to deceive is to act against the function of language which is to communicate. Lying turns language against itself. To tell a lie is to act contrary to reason. And no rational person would want to destroy language.

Evil, therefore, for Socrates is lack of proper knowledge. A thief steals because he thinks that he is doing good for himself. But he is not doing good for himself. He is acting in a way that threatens the social order upon which he himself depends. The rational question for a thief to ask is, "What will happen if everyone steals when they want something?" A social order can exist only so long as there is honesty. So Socrates insisted that a thief needs only to be shown that he is acting irrationally when he steals. In fact, a thief acts against his own rational self-interests.

Every person seeks what is good, what is right, what is true, Socrates maintained. The problem is that not everyone knows what is good, right and true. A philosopher's work is to help understand what is good, right, and true. The best way to help people see what is good, right and true is the dialectical method of asking them questions so that they will come to know and understand what is good, right and true. Asking people questions will lead them to construct answers which will eventually bring them to the truth. The result will be that people will want to live according to the standard of reason.

The Apology

A fine example of Socrates' use of reason is the account of the defence Socrates made of himself in trial when charged with sedition and atheism. The enemies of Socrates trumped up charges that he was corrupting the youth of Athens by encouraging them to question the knowledge and authority of officials and that he did not owe proper allegiance to the gods. The reason for the charges was that Socrates was seen as a threat to the new democratic government.

Plato in his account titled *The Apology* wrote that Socrates defended himself with rational arguments. He insisted that he was not a Sophist in the bad sense of the word. Rather, he insisted he was using common sense (if sense experience is unreliable, then all knowledge is suspect, he argued). He insisted that his business, his concern, was wisdom. His definition of wisdom was short: it is wisdom to not speak what one does not know; and it is wisdom not to think that one knows something which he does not know.

Socrates insisted that he was not an atheist. But he agreed to accept the punishment of death, if that was to be the vote of the citizens. He gave two reasons for the acceptance of a judgment of death against him. First, he said, it is the duty of a citizen to obey the laws of his society. And since a vote for a death sentence by Athenian citizens would follow from the laws of his city, he must abide by such a vote. And to try to flee from such a penalty, would be to disrespect the principles upon which a society is based.

Socrates maintained further that a seeker of wisdom (a philosopher) need not fear death. No living person really knows what death might entail. It is possible, Socrates insisted, that death might set a person free from the confines of the limited perspectives of time and place that confine all humans. And because no living person knows what death might be, there is no good reason to fear death.

But the citizens of Athens vote that Socrates must die.

The Crito

The arguments, given by Socrates' companions to convince Socrates to escape the death sentence, make up *The Crito*. The arguments are essentially five. Escape is an easy matter to arrange. Money is available to pay the necessary people and to allow Socrates to travel to some place such as Thessaly. Moreover, Socrates would be welcome in many places. And it is wrong to throw away one's life when it could be saved by a prudent act of self-preservation. Surely, it is right to save one's own life if it is possible to do so. In fact, not to act to save himself is to look upon himself with the same lack of respect that his accusers do. That is, if he really has something important to say and to teach, it would seem that he would be doing the right thing to save himself. Not to do so is to admit that his life and work are not worth much.

But the arguments turn personal. To not escape when he has a chance is to let down his sons. They need a father. And it is irresponsible to leave them to the care of others. His friends will suffer disgrace, since everyone expects that if Socrates really means much to his friends they will do what is necessary to let him escape execution. So the reputation of his friends is at stake, too.

Socrates' reply is the application of disinterested reason to his situation. Opinions that people hold should be taken seriously sometimes, but other times should be disregarded. It is right that we should admit and consider seriously the good opinions that people hold, but we should learn to ignore the bad opinions that people hold. And to do that is simply part of our responsibility as thinking people. In life, we know that the advice of an expert in important matters is better to seek and to follow than the advice of the unlearned or unskilled. An athlete in training follows the advice of his coach and ignores the opinions and ideas of the crowd. So we should not consider what people, in general, might think or say about our behaviour, but only to consider how an expert in right and wrong behaviour would think. And that means that opinions of ordinary people regarding escape should be ignored.

The essential question is whether or not it is right to try to escape. And that is a moral question. Issues about expenses, reputation, children are all matters reflecting the opinions of ordinary people who are generally uninformed and prone to irrational and emotional considerations.

But a rational analysis must proceed in this matter. We believe that it is bad and dishonourable to willingly do wrong, at any time. It follows that a person must not do wrong even when he is wronged by others. Just because someone does a bad and unkind thing to you, it does not mean that it is right to do a bad and unkind thing, in return.

Secondly, a person ought to fulfil the agreements made with others, provided they are proper agreements. That is, if a person commits himself to an agreement with others, it is right that he fulfils that agreement. To do, otherwise, is wrong. To try to escape, then (i.e., to leave without first persuading the court to free him) is to violate an agreement he has made with his society.

The base upon which a civil communal life rests is law. A citizen has no right to act against the laws enacted by his community, since he owes his civilized life to those laws (that is to say, the benefits of education, family and protection in a civil society follow from the laws of the community). And if a citizen does not agree with the laws of his society, he is free to leave and live somewhere else. But that also means that if a person stays in a place, he is giving agreement to the laws of the place.

To flee to a foreign country would be a foolish act. Citizens of the new country would have a right to eye him with suspicion. He betrayed the laws of his own country. What will he do with our laws, the might ask. If he could so easily avoid obligations of obedience to law in one country, surely, he could do it in another country.

Finally, Socrates asks, what are the implications of taking laws lightly? Of going against them? For one thing, no one would have good reason to pay any attention to his arguments about goodness and truthfulness if he chooses to escape and, thereby, break a law. So, Socrates concluded that he must accept the sentence of death.

The Phaedo

What is given in *The Apology* and *The Crito* is a description of what traditional philosophy is and what a philosopher does. Four principles are clear. The first is the well-known axiom that the unexamined life is not worth living. This is the claim Socrates made (and philosophers, since then, have made) that to be truly human (and, thereby, happy) a person needs to subject his or her life convictions to critical testing.

A second principle is that there are objectively valid principles of thought and action which must be followed if people are to live good lives (lives both happy and moral). A philosopher must reject the view that every person's way of life is just as good as every other person's way of life. Some people are immoral, self-indulgent, cruel, obsessed with worthless goals, confused, and blind about what is really important. And because they are confused, they are incapable of either living or of dying with any grace or dignity. Philosophers, since Socrates, don't mind saying this; and they are convinced that they have good reasons for saying this.

Yet, a third principle is that truth lies within each of us (not in the stars, or in traditions, or in religious books, or in opinions of the masses). Each person has within the true principles of right thinking and right living. In the end, therefore, no one can teach anyone else the truth about life. If the truth isn't within you, then you will never find it. If it is within, then, relentless critical self-examination will reveal it.

A fourth principle is that even though someone cannot really teach anyone else about the fundamental principles of right action and clear thinking, it is possible to ask questions that will prod people to begin the task of self-examination. These people who ask such questions are philosophers. Pilosophers ask questions to try to get others to ask questions. If a person thoughtlessly repeats traditional moral sayings of her or his society, then, the philosopher will try to force a person to question those sayings. If a person believes and asserts that everything is relative (that nothing is true and valid for all people), then the philosopher will try to force a person to question this belief.

Asking questions and forcing others to ask questions is called *the critical task of philosophy*. To be successfully critical, a person needs to study the logic of argument (so the study of logic is part of the critical side of philosophy).

But, another job of philosophy is *constructive*. One aspect of the Constructive side of philosophy is to provide answers to puzzling questions, such as "Is there anything which might survive death?" Or "Is there anything to reality which we do not and cannot ordinarily perceive?" And, then, "Is there a way to come to true conclusions about what is real, even though we cannot actually see with our eyes, feel with our fingers, such conclusions about reality?"

To answer such Constructive questions is what Socrates was trying to do in *The Phaedo*. So *The Phaedo* is an illustration of the philosophical task, both critical and constructive. But the setting of the text is important. Socrates is about to die. Why is it, Socrates asks, that a rational person should be confident that death is not something bad but something good. He answers that a philosopher practises dying, all the time.

Moreover, Socrates insisted, the soul of a person continues to exist even after death. Why might he be sure of this? Because opposite appear to produce one another. There is sleep and then there is the awakened state. There is life and, then, there is death. One is significant only in terms of the other. The two must always co-exist. But opposites do not receive or absorb one another. The stand opposite, always.

For Socrates, as we read him, as presented by Plato, the philosophical enterprise must be both analytic and constructive. Recent thinkers in the Western world have tended to accept the obligations of analysis, but have hesitated to work at the constructive side of philosophy. The constructive work of philosophy involves "metaphysics," a study of what might be thought of as a study of what is "above" or "beyond," what is known through the experiences of the senses. Metaphysical questions are those which inquire as to what makes one event follow another, always and everywhere, what is the nature of time and its inevitability, what is the nature of space that an end to it cannot be even imagined? These and more awaited the work of the philosophers, Plato and Aristotle.

10

The Ontology: Plato's Theory of Being

ONTOLOGY is the study of being. The question is "What is there to know?" "What are the possible objects of knowledge?" In short, what exists?

Plato maintained that the world of the highest reality is a non-material world of "universals" — ideas that exist prior to any specific thing or specific discovery of what is real. These pure ideas, Plato called *Forms*. These pure ideas, Forms, are unchangeable; these are what are unchanging while all else changes. For example, a specific occasion of "goodness" is a partial manifestation of the Form, "goodness."

The forms are unchanging, and they are eternal. Yet, they are also *objective essences*. That is to say, that they exist and would exist apart from any mind that might think about them. It is not necessary to have someone think about them for them to be. They are "out there" as existing things, more real than those things a person might perceive through sense perceptions.

The objects (things) that we perceive by sense experiences are related to the Forms: The forms confer reality upon the particular things known to us by sense experiences. But different objects have different relations to the Forms. Some objects might reflect a Form more clearly than others. Plato appealed to different metaphors to explain how this could be the case. For example, particular objects *embody* the Forms, that is, there might be three objects that we look at and identify as "horse" because all three embody the Form, "horse." They differ from one another in specific ways. But they are known as "horse" because they share the Form, "horse." The same could be said of "chairs." All chairs embody the Form "Chair," although they may differ in certain specific characteristics: colours may differ, some may have arms, some may have no back. But all are known as "chair" because they "participate" in the Form, "Chair."

A second metaphor, Plato employs, is the metaphor of *participation*. Objects, we see, seem to *participate* in the Forms because they exhibit the Forms, although imperfectly. And a third metaphor is to say that objects are *copies* of Forms, they are like a reflection in a mirror.

Forms relate to objects, according to Plato, in that they are separate from the objects of our sense experience, but they do not exist in an independent world. Forms are not dependent upon either objects or perceivers of objects. Yet, talk of a "World" that Forms occupy is a mistake, since by the word, "world," we must assume space and time. Talk of space and time does not apply to Forms. One might think of "triangularity." It exists nowhere, yet, it exists.

The highest, purest form is the idea of "Good." The "Good" is completely and thoroughly real. It is the source of being and substance, Plato said. As such, it is not merely a concept or an idea. The "Good" is the basis for all intelligence (Plato used the metaphor of the Sun which lights objects and makes them knowable). The Good functions in relation to forms by uniting the Forms.

The question of whether Good itself can be known or

characterized is controversial among Plato scholars. As the highest principle it has a necessary existence to tie together all aspects of reality, in Plato's scheme. But can such a general concept be known? To know, it would be to grasp it, to encompass it. The question is largely unanswered and unanswerable. And a conclusion to be drawn is that Plato's way of thinking suggests that all of our knowledge, finally, ends in mystery. Our quest for certainty of knowledge results in uncertainty.

"The Analogy of the Divided Line"

Shadows Reflections	Things/Objects	Lower Forms Mathematics	Higher Form Perfect Goodness, Justice, Beauty
A	*B*	*C*	*D*
A chair's shadow	This chair	Chair	Perfect chair

Opinion --Knowledge

A+*B* = physical world

C+*D* = world of form

C+*D* stand in the same relation as *A*+*B*, which is to say, the lower forms are but shadows of higher form.

Any shadow of this particular chair tells us *something* about this particular chair (some "shadows" tell us more than others). Thus, although the light may move and a shadow might be elongated, we can still tell it is the shadow of a chair and not the shadow of a table or of a horse. A collection, a group, of shadows may tell us more. We might photograph the shadows as the sun comes through a window at morning, noon, and late afternoon. Day after day, we could mark shadows and their successive shapes and, eventually, develop a crude science at the level of shadows, without ever seeing the actual chair. Plato's conclusion is that the relation between the sun and the chair is the same as the relations between the Form chair and a particular chair. The Form makes it a chair. It illumines "Chairness."

Now, suppose, after developing a science about chairs by looking at shadows of a chair, we were given a chance to see "the chair," itself. Then, we could say, all of those funny different shadows were actually *this Chair*. But, at various times and under different circumstances, the shadows changed shape and looked different. And, it follows, that any piece of knowledge, when we come to know it, discovers for us something else and makes something else intelligible. That new knowledge is *higher, more abstract, more significant* than the something else which is made intelligible. That bit of knowledge which is discovered, made intelligible, is lower. This is to say that the more general knowledge makes intelligible a particular bit of knowledge (once we know the chair we come to knowledge about the shadows, the shadows are made intelligible to us). A second conclusion, Plato draws, is that at the level of *Recognition* (where we see that shadows are the chairs), we are at the level of *Opinion* (not real knowledge). This is a bit like looking at the engine of my car. I recognize it as an engine, but all I could say about how to fix it would be an opinion. I cannot fix it or tell how it actually works.

Some Forms are lower than others. This means that some forms *presuppose* higher Forms (the science of geometry presupposes certain principles, such as the Euclidian axiom that parallel lines never meet). The higher a person, mentally, climbs with abstractions, the more a person frees himself from presuppositions and conditions. The highest Form Plato called *The Form of The Good*. It would be inexplicable (a mystery) for anyone who had not studied mathematics (or anyone who lived in a cave and heard only talk about a sun that lights the world). The highest knowledge is not descriptive of things out there (as scientists suppose), but is instead *intuitive* (it must be realized, experienced). Someone cannot describe it to you. And that is why Plato used myth: he could not set down in descriptive language the highest knowledge. But he was confident he could communicate it, partially, through myths, stories.

The Myth of the Sun

In the myth of the sun, Plato compared The Good to the sun. As the sun makes things on earth visible, so the Form of The Good illumines and discovers for us lower levels of knowledge and even levels of mere opinion. The sun sustains and nourishes living things. The form of the Good gives life and power to things. And, finally, there is a natural similarity between human eyes and the sun. Because we get light from the sun, we are able to see the world. In the same way, the Form of the Good satisifies questions which human minds ask. There is a mysterious relationship between human minds and The Good.

The Myth of the Cave

With another story, Plato illustrates, the human situation with regard to knowledge about what is really "real." There are people who live in a cave. There is a fire in the cave, and cave-dwellers develop a crude science, based on the shadows on the wall made by the flames. They do not know of a world, outside. They are ignorant of it. But they are happy and satisfied with their ignorance.

To convince the cave-dwellers that there is a world outside, a teacher must try to get them to turn their heads as he points outside the cave. But they have no interest in doing that. Yet, if a person were to see the what is outside the cave he would discover a whole different world from what he has known. Plato believed that there is a moral responsibility for the person who perceives reality to enter the cave and to try to convince the cave-dwellers that their "world" is not the real world. Their world is but shadows.

According to Plato, most people live in a world of shadows and are content to live that way. They do not see things as they are. And it is the duty of a philosopher to discover the real world and to show that real world to ordinary people.

11

Plato and Art

THERE is no comprehensive theory of art contained in the works by Plato, available to readers today. He did write some things about art. And he implied many things about art.

If we look at what Plato said about art, we get a very negative view of art (art is phoney, art deceives, art is, in fact, dangerous for a society). But it is necessary to admit that Plato did his own art when he created myths to illustrate his ideas. So it must be admitted that there is a value to art in the thought of Plato.

Plato's negative assessment of art follows from his theory of being and from his theory of knowledge. We recognize beautiful things by their participation in the ideal Form, "Beauty." In the same manner, we recognize one horse, Dobbin, to be a horse, because it participates in the general concept of "Horseness," and so, we recognize any beautiful thing, to be beautiful, because it participates in the general Form, "Beauty."

But looking at particular objects of beauty gives a very inadequate knowledge of beauty, in the same way, that looking at just one horse, Dobbin, provides little information about all horses or about the Form, "Horseness."

Works of art are very much removed from the Form, "Beauty," because works of art are copies of some particular thing that participates in the Form, "beauty" (art is a copy of a copy, therefore). An artist in drawing or painting what strikes him or her as a beautiful scene in nature copies (puts on canvas) what is seen. In this sense, art is an imitation of a particular thing. But, since the artist is copying things which, themselves, are, once, removed from real beauty (they are only approximations of the Form, "Beauty"), the artist is, in a sense, actually, something of a liar and deceiver. The artist is not telling the truth about something. The artist is making a copy of a copy. And this means that art cannot communicate truth. Art fails, when it tries to communicate truth. And, since, most art appeals to our emotions, our feelings, art is a social menace if it falls into the hands of the wrong people.

A more positive assessment of art follows from Plato's own use of art, as narrative. He uses both myth and allegory. Allegory appears in Plato as something of a short-cut or substitute. But allegory, in Plato's hands, is a creative use of words to illustrate an abstract concept. As a short-cut, or substitute, Plato, over and over again, uses allegory as a way to make a point.

Allegory, in the hands of Plato, is a creative use of words to illustrate an abstract concept. He uses some concrete, particular thing to illustrate and point to abstract concepts. Allegory and myth, therefore, are creative acts, a condensation of a complex meaning or experience into concrete, specific incidents and occurrences. This is to say that a literary artist is attempting to improve upon nature or upon words (the artist clarifies our sense of reality by ordering our experiences of it).

An example of what Plato did with allegory might be the analogy of the difference between experience and cognition. Knowing what it means to be on a ship under attack is possible only to someone who has had the actual experience. No description, however accurate, can duplicate the actual experience (the knowing) of that sort of an event. A civilian reading an account in a newspaper or a staff officer at headquarters knows nothing comparable to what a survivor of such an experience knows.

On the other hand, a sailor under attack often does not know what has happened to the ship, what has actually occurred, or what has happened to his shipmates. A sailor on the attacked ship is, too, overwhelmed by the immediacy of his experience to understand it or to put it all into a larger context. A person, experiencing something like a naval attack, is much like a person whose sensory apparatus is overloaded and overwhelmed and, then, deadened by shock. So, from this point of view, a civilian reading a carefully detailed newspaper account *knows more* than the man having the experience. Or, a staff officer at headquarters who knows the location of the ship, the logistics of enemy movement in the water, the extent of damage involved, *knows more* than the man undergoing the experience.

An artist, in this sense, is a person who stands between the two levels of knowing and tries to provide both the *experience* and the *objective distance* needed to provide a complete knowledge of a situation. An artist *imitates* as accurately as possible the actual experience. But an artist also maintains a distance from the experience to provide a more complete perspective of the experience. We might say that Plato seems to want the artist to give an idealized portrayal of reality. The artist, thus, provides objectivity, perspective and universality, at the same time, as he provides a direct, immediate experience.

Idealization in the Parthenon

The parthenon, as an architectural monument, is a work which unites the geometric exactness of post-lintel construction with the reality of the actual experience a person, observing the structure, has. The temple building, dedicated to the goddess Athena, is a simple box-like structure using post-lintel technique to enclose a space. Over the top of the structure, the architect placed a triangular prism for a roof. The architect brought together the perfect geometric form of a box with a prism on top of it.

But, to create a perception of a perfect box and a prism, the architect deviated from the perfect geometric forms of box and prism. The columns are more slender at the top than at the bottom. There is an outward curvature of the columns (*entasis*). The cornice is not, in fact, a straight line; it is higher at the middle than at each end. The sides of the triangular pediment curve. The base upon which the columns rest is higher at the middle than at the ends. The columns are not vertical but slant inward about 2½ inches. The entablature leans outward. The columns on the peristyle are not an equal distant from one another (the columns at the corners are two feet closer to their neighbours). And the corner columns are wider than the inner columns. The architect, as an artist, created an illusion of perfection. By abandoning geometric exactness, the architect created distortion (according to exact measurement) but optical precision for the observer.

Possibly, the same things could be said about the adjustments to a well-known story which Aeschylus makes in order to tell again the Agamemnon story (or Sophocles re-telling the Oedipus story). An artist, creatively, adjusts what is given in direct experience to make something more perfect. And that is art. That is creativity.

12

Aristotle (384-322 BC)

ARISTOTLE was a student of Plato at Athens. For more than twenty years, he studied with Plato. But, in 342 BC, Aristotle was recalled to Macedonia (his birthplace) by king Philip of Macedon to be the tutor for Philip's son, Alexander (who became "Alexander the Great"). When Aristotle returned to Athens, he began a school of philo-sophy, which came to be known as the *Peripatetic School*, because of his habit of walking, while conversing with his students.

Aristotle's teachings, eventually, became diametrically opposed to Plato in many ways. Plato was interested in ideas; Aristotle was interested in things. And Aristotle insisted that ideas do not have an existence of their own (they are not independent things). Ideas, he maintained, are derived from concrete experiences. Plato could say, for example, that if all people died, the idea of people would still remain. Aristotle insisted that there are only individual people (a man or a woman) and the generalization (people) is created by our experience of individual people.

Aristotle's interest in starting study with particular things led him to the study of "particulars." In one sense, then, it could be said that Aristotle is the first real scientist, the first to seriously examine and to categorize things of biology, physics, astronomy and more. The "Aristotelian urge" was to connect isolated facts and to derive some general rules from particular cases. His view was that the inquisitive mind should move from particular things, particular instances, to generalizations about those. And he developed a powerful tool to assist him in doing that — logic.

Aristotle's logic is a rigorous, consistent and intellectually honest system of classification and analysis of relations. It is from Aristotle that we get the basis for what we can think of as *Rational Law*. There are three laws of logic which are built into the structure of the universe, Aristotle maintained. One is the Law of *Identity*, which asserts, simply, that if a statement is true, then, it is true. The second is the law of *Contradiction*: no statement can be both true and false. And the third is the law of the *Excluded Middle*: A proposition (a statement that something is the case) is either true or it is false.

The typical form in which Aristotle constructed logical arguments was the *syllogism* (we might say he "discovered" it). The syllogism consists of a *major premise,* a *minor premise* and a *conclusion,* which follows necessarily from the major and minor premises. An example might be the following argument: *Major premise,* That all art is creative; *Minor premise,* That sculpture is an art; *Conclusion,* Therefore sculpture is creative. The famous argument is *All men are mortal; Socrates is a man; Therefore, Socrates is mortal.*

The Syllogism must be formed properly or it will draw an "invalid" conclusion (conclusions are either "valid" or "invalid" in logical discourse not *True or False*). And example might be *Major premise*: All cows eat grass; *Minor premise*: This man eats grass; *Invalid conclusion*: Therefore this man is a cow. If all cows are animals that eat grass, it does not follow that all animals that eat grass are cows (All *X* is *Y* does not mean that All *Y* is *X*).

Aristotle is also notable for the distinction he drew between *Matter* and *Form*. Matter, Aristotle said, is just that, it is an unstructured, undifferentiated glob of stuff. Form is what makes matter identifiable, classifiable, knowable. An artist (a sculptor) creates a form out of a lump of clay (matter). *The processes* of the universe are created from out of the prime matter of the universe. Those processes might be evolution. They might be God's creative powers.

The Major Works of Aristotle

One major work is the *Organon*, an examination of logic, the "science" of reasoning. In this text, Aristotle writes of the *Syllogism*. And it must be admitted that, later, philosophers added little to what Aristotle put on paper.

With *On Metaphysics* (Aristotle himself used the term *prote philosophia*, "first philosophy" to imply that metaphysics is basic, most important. Metaphysics, he maintained, is the study of what is most real, what is the essential substance of the universe. It is in this work that he makes the essential distinction between Matter and Form. At the lowest end of the scale of reality there is "formless matter" which has no real existence but only logical existence. And, at the highest level, there must exist a Prime Form which is free from matter and which gives "Form" to the universe. This he identifies to be God. Aristotle's idea of Form differs from Plato's idea of Form. And it gives credence to his idea of God. For Aristotle, Form makes something what it is. It exists in a thing. And that, it would seem, makes Prime Form existent in all things.

On Natural Philosophy (Physica, De caelo, De generatione et corruptione, Meteorologica)

In the *Physica*, Aristotle gives what are the Four Causes of anything. *Material Cause* is that out of which a thing comes to be. A *Formal Cause* is the intelligible nature of a thing, that is, in which it is made to be what it is. A *Moving Cause* is that cause which immediately brings change. And a *Final Cause* is the end or aim or purpose of the change, brought by causation.

Ethics and Politics (Nicomachean Ethics and the Eudemian Ethics)

For Aristotle, ethics is a branch of politics. All people are members of a society. So, a most important political question is an ethical question: how should people live well, together?

Aristotle argued that the aim of life is happiness (*eudaimonia*) — not pleasure, not honour, not wealth. And the highest happiness, he insisted, is Contemplation, a rational contemplation of philosophic truth. Ordinary people are, probably, incapable of such contemplation, so they must settle for a happiness which is to be found in morality and practical wisdom. Wisdom in morality would provide an ordinary person a disposition to choose between ways of acting that would avoid extremes of conduct. This is to live according to *The Golden Mean*. The disposition encourages a behaviour which would neither slam the door when angry nor drink too much when happy.

Such talk continues with *Politica* (The Politics). The city-state, Aristotle argued, is the best organization for people. It provides the best social environment for a person to develop personal capacities that lead to happiness. Because the *moral development* of people is the chief end of the state, it is important that power should rest not with the wealthy or with the general populace, but with the good people. Aristotle recognized that there are certain advantages to democracy, but he found that the best government would be a monarchy or the perfect ruler. And if a perfect ruler is not available, then an aristocracy of men of morality and rationality should rule. But, finding an enlightened aristocracy might be difficult. So a *limited democracy* is, probably, the best, given the way things are (this is to say, the democracy should be limited to those people who have some capacity by intelligence and morality to rule). How to find such people remains a difficulty.

Aristotle regarded slavery as natural. Some people are by nature fools without sufficient intelligence to live well on their own. So slavery should be based on the nature of the inferiority of some people, not on conquest by warfare or any other means. And a master should always provide hope for the liberation of a slave (that is, a master should do what can be done to improve the mental and moral capacity of slaves so that they might be given freedom). Slavery is a matter of inferiority.

Aristotle's *On Rhetoric and Poetry* is concerned with the methods of persuasion, if a person might be employed as a lecturer or speaker. Three methods might be employed. One is to produce a favourable impression about one's own characster. A second is a method to produce certain emotions in an audience. And a third is a method to argue rationally to convince an audience about some matter (this might entail providing an example or by using the syllogism).

13

Hellenistic and Roman Thought

THE conquests of Alexander the Great marked a great epoch in history. The distinct culture of the Greek city-states was spread throughout the East as far as India. Alexander (and his successors) encouraged large numbers of Greeks to move in order to populate and to develop new Greek cities of the East. Those Greeks that encountered new people and new cultures, went through what we might call a cultural crisis.

The old city-state ways didn't work in the greatly expanded new world. A sense of order, that had guided and held together the city-states no longer could exist in the much wider world. One result was confusion, political, social and moral. It was not until the rule of the Roman Emperor Augustus (27-14 BC) that stability was established.

Some later Greek philosophers had thought it necessary to step into the situation of disorder in the region and to make some sense of it (that is, philosophy for the Greeks was a matter of social relevance). Two great philosophical movements took shape: Epicureanism and Stoicism. But there also appeared philosophers we know as Cynics.

The teachings of Epicureanism and Stoicism were chiefly ethical in the sense that both movements encouraged people to rise above the temptations for sensuality and greed that new opportunities provided (that is, there was built into the teachings of both movements an encouragement toward a moral life as the best life to live). Both movements taught that a discovery of self-sufficiency, independence, and freedom was what a person needed most. Philosophy was seen as a way to find some purpose to life — some sense of control over one's fate in what was increasingly thought by people to be a dangerous, uncertain, and, indeed, risky world. In this sense, Stoicism, Epicureanism, and Cynicism all showed an affinity to the interests of those Hindu thinkers who were sceptical of "common sense worldly" values and commitments. At the same time, one might find Stoic thinkers to be welcome today.

All of these thinkers seemed to be in agreement that a good life might be found if a person's field of interest were reduced significantly. In other words, a withdrawal from ordinary life was encouraged. Individual philosophers disagreed with one another about exactly what a person should focus upon to bring about a withdrawal from the world. But an important theme among them all was to put a high value upon learning to control the effects of the outer world upon oneself. Here again, an affinity to Indian Hindu and Buddhist thinkers is to be noted. Wisdom, it was agreed, had to do with gaining control over passions, emotions, feelings. The goal was to find a sense of independence from those external things which might bring unhappiness, worry, pain.

Three Philosophical Movements: Cynics (Sceptics), Stoics, Epicureans

"Cynic," from the Greek *kunos*, means "dog-like" and is related to the word "canine." Teles, Antisthenes, and Diogenes, are representative Cynic thinkers. One might not expect it, but the teaching was a philosophy of consolation.

The general approach of all Cynic thinkers was to call into question the older values of the Greek city-states. But, as well, the teachings were a prescription for behaviour for any whose lives had become intolerable because of the collapse of the world about them or for reasons of personal despair. A general view was that the trappings of culture are worthless: government, private property, marriage, religion, luxuries, and pleasures of the senses are actually traps which make life more miserable. If there is any hope for people, it is to be found in a rejection of society and in a return to a simple life of asceticism, self-denial, self-mortification.

The Cynics believed that the world was fundamentally evil; in order to live properly a person must withdraw from participation in it. Teles, for example, insisted that ordinary living was governed, controlled, by attachments to possessions and to other people, such as family and friends. The trouble with attachments to things and people is that attachment creates dependencies, which, in turn, bring all sorts of trouble into life and, finally, will put people at the mercy of things external (things over which people can have no control).

The way to secure independence from these outside forces (matters external to the private self) is to simply abolish any interest in them. Possessions, for example: Rich people actually do not use a large number of the things they possess. What profit is it to possess them, then? A slave gets on well enough without someone to wait on him; why should not the slave's independence in this matter be the free man's independence also?

As for food, the roadsides and byways offer growing plants which can be eaten, and there are springs of water everywhere. Why do old women sing as they bake barley cakes and carry water? They sing because they are independent. And clothing: There is no need to seek a thicker coat in cold weather. Simply, fold your present coat, and there you will have a garment of double thickness. And, it is best not to be troubled by other people. The person who has many people about him must constantly worry about political order, social life, financial matters, and on and on.

And the same must be said for children and friends. It is best not to tie oneself down with either. Children and friends create worries that cannot be successfully resolved.

But if riches should happen to fall your way, that is okay. Teles, for example, did not insist that a person renounce wealth. Instead, one should accept what enjoyments that might occur. But a person must avoid *dependence* upon those things which might bring brief happiness.

Antisthenes dressed like a workman, took no pay for his teaching, and perferred to take poor people for his pupils. Anyone unwilling to practise poverty and hardship he drove away with his club. Diogenes was a bankrupt banker. He was so poor that he had to beg. He was pleased to take the view that begging was a good and moral and wise thing to do. He wore beggar's clothes, and, for a time, made his home in a tub in the court of a temple at Athens. He taught that the simple life of animals is best. He slept on the ground, ate whatever he could find wherever he found it, and performed the duties of nature and the joys of lovemaking in the sight of everyone and anyone. He injured no one, but refused to recognize laws, and announced himself a citizen of the world. He lived the simple life so consistently that he became the most famous man in Greece, next to Alexander, the Great.

Maybe all the world knows the story of Alexander coming upon Diogenes, lying on the ground warming himself in the sun. "I am Alexander the Great, King," Alexander said. "Ask of me any favour you choose." Replied Diogenes, "Stand out of the sunlight, you are casting a shadow on me." Alexander allegedly said, "If I were not Alexander, I would be Diogenes." Diogenes did not return the compliment (in short, he had no interest in being Alexander the Great).

Cynicism was decidedly anti-social. The teaching did not attempt to describe how people might be happy as social beings, but it encouraged people to find individual salvation. In this sense, Cynicism was one of the forerunners of various ascetic movements that appeared during Hellenistic times. The ascetic movements encouraged isolated, solitary living, fasting, subjecting the self to physical and mental discomfort. The moral teaching was this: eat as little as possible; possess only the bare essentials to keep yourself alive; desire nothing; drink only water; injure no one.

A cynic would not marry: but cynics did patronize prostitutes. Diogenes advocated free love and what might be thought of as a community of wives: women should be shared by the men of a community. And cynics could not understand why it was that it was appropriate for a man to satisfy his appetite for food in public but inappropriate to satisfy his appetite for sex in public.

Cynicism had some influence in the development of early Christian philosophy: a monk could be seen as someone who followed the advice of the Cynic when he lived a simple, frugal, cloistered life, shunning conventional social values concerning property, marriage, and fame. In short, many of the negative views of the Cynics were adopted by some early Christians — especially, those that promoted austerity in living. Cynicism might be characterized as "other worldly" in its emphasis upon rejecting conventional social values.

Stoicism

Zeno founded the Stoic school of thought in 301 BC in Athens. Later Stoics were Epictetus, Cicero, and Marcus Aurelius, a Roman emperor. It is fair to describe Stoicism as the most influential ethical teaching of the ancient Western world before Christianity. The teaching swept over Greece after Alexander's death, and it dominated Roman thought until Christianity became an important ethical teaching. Stoicism, like Cynicism, was very much a result of the uncertainty and dismay which afflicted many thinkers after the collapse of the city-states and the growth and collapse of the Empire of Alexander. Stoics, like Cynics, were convinced that no reconstruction of past greatness was possible. The teaching, therefore, consists of advice to individuals. The teaching maintained that only individual, private, happiness might be obtained when a social order is crumbling.

Zeno (not the Zeno of Elea, the originator of the famous logical paradoxes) lectured in the third century BC, usually from the porch of a building. The Greek word for porch is *stoa*. And the teaching associated with Zeno's porch lectures became known as Stoicism.

Epictetus (who began life as a slave, but then rose to be an official in the Roman government) wrote a famous treatise titled "Progress or Improvement." He maintained that some people have power over the external matters that affect individuals (these people can control matters from the general economy to decisions about who should be put in prison or made a slave). But such people are few in number. Most people are out of control of their lives. And their only hope is to become indifferent to the threats of external events, that might affect them. By practising indifference a person can become independent of the world and free of its unhappy occurrences. In short, a person can have a good life if he can learn simply to accept what happens. Any person who struggles to change things (to make things better) is going to be miserably unhappy. One is smartest to cultivate detachment from the world. Stoicism exhibits, at this point, similarities to Hindu and Buddhist practice, both of which put great emphasis upon freedom from the external world.

Stoicism differed in, at least, one important way from Cynicism (and from Hindu and Buddhist thoughts): one need not renounce involvement with the world. A person need only to learn *indifference*. This meant that a Stoic could live a life of pleasure or of political responsibility. The essential and necessary factor in each case is to cultivate indifference toward success or failure. In fact, many Stoic thinkers insisted that a person must do the duty that falls to oneself and avoid attachment and dependence. Do not seek public office. But if public office comes in the course of doing one's duty, it should not be avoided. The key is to cultivate indifference. A main consequence of this ethical teaching was to place responsibility for a good life or a bad life, directly upon the individual and not upon society or family. A person needs to cultivate a frame of mind which makes him indifferent to the usual affairs of the world.

A major move of the Stoic thinkers was the teaching about the nature of reason. Stoic thinkers insisted that the natural world is ordered according to rational principles (there is a rational order to nature). Events do not happen randomly. There is an order to the way things happen. The principle of order is *Logos* (Reason).

For example, the principles of rationality hold everywhere. The rational Law of Identity is that if a statement is true, then, it is true (and it is to break with reason to regard it as false). The rational Law of Contradiction holds, everywhere: no statement can be both true and false. The rational Law of the Excluded Middle is the case, everywhere: a proposition is either true and false. The principle of *Logos* was regarded by some as God, Providence (in the sense, that there is a reason for all events). The principle was regarded by others as Nature (all things are the same, in the sense that they fall under the principle of rational order).

Implications for such ideas are important. All people are equally under the universal law of rationality (i.e., 2+2 cannot be 5, somewhere in the world). In this sense, Reason and Nature are fundamentally of equal status (what is happening in nature corresponds to the natural law of reason). Reason, Nature, and Rational Necessity are equated (what is happening in nature must happen, the way it happens, as a matter of the rational order of things). Human beings are unique rational animals who can know and understand the logic of the universe. But the logical order of nature stands in contrast to the emotions, feelings, inclinations of people.

Certain ethical principles follow from this. One's first duty is to submit to the law of Reason. But, few people in the world do this. Most people are motivated in their actions by self-interest, emotion, or greed. So, a person is not likely to be able to do much about what others might be doing. A person, nevertheless, can do something about the effects of what others do. Reason instructs that one must overcome the world outside of oneself by overcoming dependence upon other people and their actions. Duty to oneself is to discover rationality within oneself (development of the mind toward independence, rational control, indeed, asceticism will occur by attention to reason).

Epicureanism

Epicurus, a Greek (died 270 BC (?)) and Lucretius, a Roman (died 55 BC (?)) were the major thinkers of this school of ancient thought. Lucretius' book *The Nature of the Universe* is a major surviving text. In short, the teachings hold that the chief goal of life should be to avoid pain and to seek pleasure. These thinkers put as much stress on the first part of the proposition as on the second. Political ambition, pursuit of wealth, physical pleasures, in the end, always cause more pain than they are worth, these men held. So, the wise person will find happiness by living a careful life of proper conduct (which will be the practice of moderation in all things).

Lucretius, in his book, argued for Materialism, Atheism, and Hedonism. Materialism, for Lucretius, meant that nature is self-contained, self-regulating and self-explanatory. And, he provided a theory to show that what makes up the things of nature can be explained by matter interacting with matter. He maintained that the components of matter are atoms. All events, all happenings in the world, can be explained by some natural, material cause. Material things consist, ultimately, of atoms and compounds of atoms. An atom is indivisible and indestructible.

There is such a thing as space and space must be infinite,

he maintained. We see things moving and since motion requires space, there must be such a thing as empty space, in which things move. But space is infinite because a boundary to space is inconceivable. Space cannot have a limit unless there is something outside of it to limit it. That would be to say that something else takes up space. Thus, an end to space is rationally inconceivable.

For both Epicurus and for Lucretius, atheism is a practical atheism. God is irrelevant. Much of the pain and suffering in the world results from an incorrect belief that supernatural forces have some control over the life and destiny of human beings. In his work, Lucretius cites Agamemnon's stupid act of killing his daughter, Iphigenia, because of superstitious belief in gods. And that was the act that messed up his life and resulted in his own death.

Further, if Materialism is the case, the idea of the immortality of the soul is superstition, as well. What we might call *spirit* is known only in conjunction with the body (we do not know of disembodied spirits). If the spirit is immortal, then it must possess, as well, the five senses (but the five senses are part of the body, they are material). But, we cannot imagine a spirit without that spirit having sense perceptions. And, it is ludicrous to suppose that spirits are standing by at the mating and birth of humans, jostling and scrambling to get, in first, and establish themselves, firmly in a body. It is far more rational to assume that what is called spirit is simply the joining of the body and mind (and when the body dies, there can be no loner "spirit" that joins the two). The conclusion, to be drawn, is that death is no threat. Once a person accepts the inevitability of death, then, that person is free from fear and anxiety about death.

It follows that the proper aim of life is to maximize pleasure and to reduce pain. But, for Epicurus and Lucretius, the pursuit of real pleasure requires the avoidance of pain. And, since some pleasures result in pain, not all pleasures are to be pursued. So, pleasures must be studied. And they can be classified. There are Natural and Necessary desires of the body, such as desires for food and sleep. But there are also Natural and unnecessary desires, such as desire for sexual pleasure. And there are wholly Unnatural Desires, desires for exotic food, expensive, showy possessions and luxuries.

The Natural and Necessary desires must be satisfied or there will be undesirable consequences. Unnatural desires do not have to be satisfied (for the simple reason that they are unnatural). Whereas there is a termination to natural desires (the desire for food ends when the stomach is full), unnatural desires have no such natural limit (attempts to fulfil unnatural desires merely expands them). The chief natural desire is *Repose*, both mental and physical.

Epicurean ethical thought has been criticized. The teaching implies that ordinary moral virtues are really good and worth cultivating only if they serve as a means to the end of pleasure as repose. If, however, it might be the case that a clever man can produce more pleasure than pain by dishonesty, then, it seems a person should do so. An Epicurean must be able to show that honesty, for example, will, in the end, really produce more pleasure for a person. Otherwise, it follows that the pursuit of dishonesty (or some other vice) might be justified by its usefulness in providing the pleasure of Repose.

A student, educated in Indian thought, might wonder whether Cynic, Stoic and Epicurean thinkers might have been influenced by traditions of India. The themes of renunciation, of isolation, of freedom, all, suggest similarities, which seem more than accidental. How to trace such a connection between the West and the East remains today a problem. Scholars such as Mircea Eliade and Joseph Campbell showed remarkable similarities in the mythologies of the West and the East. More work is to be done with surviving documents of major constructive philosophers.

14

Hebrew People and Hebrew Religion

To study the Hebrew people is to study a people, who, for centuries, have been known as Jews. Such a name dates from the so-called *Diaspora* ("Dispersion") of some of the Hebrew people from their homeland on the east side of the Mediterranean Sea. The *Diaspora* is dated at 586 BC, the date of the defeat and subsequent captivity of the so-called Southern Kingdom of Judah by Babylonian forces. The Northern kingdom of Hebrews ("Israel") had suffered defeat some two hundred years, earlier, when Assyrian armies invaded their territories. Efforts to trace the history of the conquered people of the north have been futile.

In phases, a remnant of Judah managed to return from Babylon beginning in 536 BC. The return to the land they believed to be theirs was not a simple matter, however. Repossessing territories from a population accustomed to ownership proved difficult. And the story of these people is a story of a struggle for land. The struggle continues even today. The people of Judah (known as "Jews" — children of Judah) today work to maintain a nation called Israel in territory for which they insist they hold a historic right. And, again, they must take from others a land, they claim their god gave them.

A historical consideration of these people, who have come through history as Jews, then, is of significance for an understanding of the past as well as contemporary events in the Middle East. It will be clear that disagreements, controversies and resentments run deep. At the base of the matter is land, territory, property. Who has a right to what territory?

The History of Jews in the Biblical Era

The major source for the study of the people, known as Jews, is the Hebrew *Bible*. It is a book regarded by Jews to be not only a historical record but a sacred text, as well. Questions of authenticity and historical accuracy might trouble a modern reader. But, Jews tie themselves to the book. Some even insist that it must be read and interpreted as a historically accurate text. A more moderate view maintains that it is a book written by Jews about what Jews claim to be their history. Some incidents and events can be corroborated by independent scholars of history. Other incidents and events must be regarded with the same mind used when reading of Odysseus' descent into the underworld for conversations with the dead Agamemnon and others.

The destruction of the temple in Jerusalem in 586 BCE is thought by many to be a crucial event for the self-understanding of Jewish people. A sense of being a distinct people having a particular history and a tradition rises to significance in the texts being written. And that tradition and history became a major theme of the scripture.

The Patriarchal Period

Seven periods mark the history given in the scripture. The first is labelled *The Partriarchal Period* and it is covered in chapters 12-50 of the first book called "Genesis." The story begins with a man, named Abram, who left Ur of the

Chaldees (a city and cultural centre near the Tigris and Euphrates River area) because he believed that God had told him to do so. The story says that God promised Abram a land and a great people (which would "number more than the sands of the sea"). Abram left Ur of the Chaldees and headed west towards, what is labelled in the text as Canaan (later, known as Palestine). The stories recorded in the "Book of Genesis" are of the so-called patriarchs (the fathers of the Jewish faith).

Abram eventually changed his name to Abraham. And, because of his wife's fertility-difficulties, he sired a son by means of his wife's servant. That son he named Ishmael. Sarah, his wife, was unhappy with the matter of surrogacy, and, after repeated attempts at conception, she did bear a son. She named him Isaac. The unhappiness of Sarah resulted in the banishment of the servant woman and her son, Ishmael. There are some in the Middle East today who trace their ancestry to Ishmael.

Isaac had two sons of his own after marriage — Esau and Jacob. Esau, being the eldest son, stood in line for what was thought to be the promise of greatness given to Abraham. But, Jacob managed to trick the old and blind Isaac into giving him the ceremonial blessing of successor to Abraham. Jacob sired twelve sons. And he changed his name to Israel.

The stories give some attention to geographical detail that has been confirmed by archeological evidence. That is, evidence indicates the presence of people in the areas the texts name. Yet, the stories were written some time after the events took place. So, maybe more is to be learned about the people writing the stories than the ancient history talked about in the stories.

The Egyptian Period and the Exodus

Some of the descendants of Jacob (Israel) moved to Egypt. Eventually these people were made slaves, the text says. But under the leadership of a man named Moses, they escaped from slavery and tried to return to Palestine area. The return journey was difficult (recalled in the later writings as "the period of wandering in the desert"), but finally, under the leadership of Joshua, they crossed the Jordan river and entered territory they thought to be theirs. They believed that the land (referred to in the text as Canaan) was theirs as a gift from their god.

The exodus (exit) from Egypt is dated around 1300 BC. From this experience of escape from slavery, two important ideas of lasting significance emerged. One is the idea of convenant. The people began to believe that they escaped from slavery because of a special relationship they held with their god. Their god had established a covenant with Abraham, their forefather, they believed, and he was confirming that agreement by rescuing them from slavery in Egypt.

Covenant relationships are special relationships. A covenant is like a contract relationship, in some ways, but it differs, too. A covenant binds a *complete person* into a complete relationship. One might have a contract relationship to perform a particular service. And, aside from the service, the contracted person is free and independent. *Covenant*, on the other hand, binds a person completely and totally (a person has a "covenant" in a marriage relationship which makes it a full-time commitment). Jews began to interpret their past history in terms of the covenant relationship which they believe was established with Abraham. Because of the covenant, as a people they had a close and binding relationship to the god of Abraham, Isaac and Jacob.

A second significant idea, that followed from the exodus from slavery, was the notion of *Law* (*Torah*). Climbing to the desert-mount named Sinai, Moses received from their god the laws for the people. The Law laid out boundaries of proper behaviour. The legal idea seems to be that people were free to do many things, but that there were boundaries which the law established: the words are negative assertions. "Thou shall not" preface the ten laws ("The Decalogue"). In short, a person is free to perform a range of actions, but a person must not step over the boundary. "Thou shall not steal" meant that a person was free to drive a hard bargain, but a person was not to take what does not belong to him. "Thou shall not commit adultery" was taken to mean that a man might love many women, but he is not to take another man's wife. In short, there is a range of acceptable behaviour, but there is a boundary which should not be crossed. A typical form of punishment was stoning: a person who stepped over the boundary was to be taken *outside the camp* and killed by having rocks hurled at him or her. Stoning, performed away from "the camp," symbolized the consequence of crossing a boundary.

The Period of Conquest and the Judges

The people moved through territory on the east side of the Jordan River. Eventually, they made a quick entrance into "the promised land" by crossing the river. But, the people experienced difficulties in establishing themselves, there. They were, of course, regarded as invaders by the Canaanites. And, these people were not warm to the idea that the Jewish god could give away their land. Moreover, organization of the people was a problem. A general organizational scheme divided the people into "tribes," that denoted an ancestral connection to one of the twelve sons of Jacob (Israel). Each of the tribes claimed a section of the land. So there was the region of Judah, the region of Benjamin, the region of Reuben, etc. Establishing possession of a territory was difficult. And, leadership was spontaneous and erratic, having mostly to do with crisis-situations of aggressive animosity from Canaanites. People who appeared as leaders were known as Judges. Samson, Gideon and even an occasional woman such as Deborah, became leaders who could inspire the disparate populations of the tribes. The text of the *Book of the Judges* suggests that there was a great deal of chaos in the land, chaos among Jews and Canaanites. A phrase occurring again and again in the text is "and everyone did that which was right in his own eyes."

The Period of the Hebrew Monarchy

Books of *Samuel, Kings* and *Chronicles* tell of the establishment of a Hebrew monarchy. The concentrated resistance from the indigenous populations as well as requirements for tighter organization forced a move toward finding a king to lead the people. A man named Saul was elected to serve as king. The position was a permanent office (Saul was king for life). Yet, the office was not thought to be hereditary: Saul's sons competed with one another for the position of a successor to their father. But the second king was selected by god, it was thought: David, a fairly insignificant sheep-herder was appointed king by an honoured prophet. The new king moved the capital city to Jerusalem. And he extended the empire in every direction. Diplomatic relations with kings in surrounding territories were established (generally by traditional means of the harem).

King David was succeeded by his son, Solomon. Rather than extend the territory, Solomon turned his attention to the economy. He divided the land into twelve taxable districts, constructed a temple for the worship of the god of the Hebrew people, and built a luxurious palace for himself and his household.

The Period of the Divided Kingdom

The Books of the Kings (two books) tell the story of the division of the kingdom. Rheoboam, a son, took the throne at Solomon's death. Many were unhappy with the heavy taxation. But, when people asked Rheoboam for tax relief he refused, became angry because they asked, and laid upon them additional taxes. Some people revolted; and ten of the tribes selected Jereboam (another son of Solomon) to be their king. These people took the name Israel as the name of their kingdom. They are known to the texts as the Northern Kingdom, whereas Judah was the Southern Kingdom.

The Northern Kingdom survived until 721 BC. Assyria invaded from the north and east, took leaders captive and the remaining people were absorbed by non-Jewish settlers or indigenous people. The Northern Kingdom (Israel) was much influenced by local religions associated with fertility worship. The worship was centred around Baal-Melkart, a Syrian god associated with agriculture and fertility. The stories of the prophets, Elijah and Elisha concern these troubles in the north.

The Southern Kingdom (Judah) managed to survive independently until 586 BC. At that time, Babylon of the

Tigris/Euphrates River region, conquered Palestine and took as captives the leading families of Judah (the Babylonians destroyed the palace as well as the so-called Temple of Solomon).

The Period of the Exile

The term, *exile*, refers to the period during which both Judah and Israel are out of the land of Palestine. Only the people of Judah returned to the land, however. During the exile, the people were without a temple. So they developed what is known today as *synagogue* with a *rabbi*, a teacher, as the major religious authority. During the time of exile there was much questioning concerning why they had been taken from the land which they believed had been given to them because of the covenant. Why? For what reasons? many asked.

So exile, captivity, sharpened the spiritual concern of some Jews. What is known to scholars as the "deuteronomic view of history" was developed, at this time: it is the view that historical events concerning the Jews indicate the favour or the displeasure of their god. In short, what happened to the Jews happened because the people had misconstrued, misinterpreted or mismanaged the covenant relationship.

The Post-Exile Period

The Babylonian Empire collapsed in 539 BC. Cyrus the Great, a Persian, conquered and ruled the region. Cyrus, then allowed some Jews to return to Palestine in 536 BC. Those that returned found little to be happy about, since the temple had been destroyed and those Jews that had remained there had neglected the faith.

Two men, Zechariah and Haggai, inspired the people

to re-build the temple. This was completed by 515 BC. The story of their efforts is found in two books of Jewish scripture bearing their names, *Zechariah* and *Haggai*. And, it is these two books that the biblical story of the Jews ends.

The Persian Empire weakened and the Greek Empire under Alexander rose to prominence. Palestine was conquered by the Greeks and the Jews were ruled and reduced to near slavery once again. But, this time they were slaves in their own land.

Then the Romans rose to power. They, too, took control of Palestine and ruled the Jews. As a response to domination by foreign powers, Jews split into some significant groups. A group known as Zealots was fanatic Jews who insisted that the territory was theirs as a gift from their god. They advocated terrorist activities against the occupying Roman forces as well as against those Jews who were thought to be compromising the covenant by collaborating with Romans.

A second group that appeared at this time was the Essenes. These people maintained that domination by foreigners was happening because Jews were not serious about the covenant. These moved out of the cities to the deserts and lived celibate lives, devoted to meditation and prayer.

A third group was known as Sadducees. These were priest who conducted the rituals at the re-constructed temple. But, in order to practise the rituals effectively, many advocated open recognition of the validity of Roman rule. The rationale for peace with the rulers was the view that religion and government were separate and distinct concerns. In short, if the government would stay out of religion, religion would stay out of government.

And a fourth group was the Pharisees. This party contended with the Sadducees for the favour of ordinary Jewish people. These received bad treatment by writers of the early Christian documents. But, the fact of the matter is that they did represent the interests of ordinary people against the elitism of the priestly aristocracy of Sadducees.

Some Important Ideas from the Biblical Period

An important idea is that of a creator, god. The biblical text traces the story of the Jewish people, back to creation. The god of the Jews, the text implies, is the god of all creation. The name of the god was too holy to be written. But occasionally, four letters of the Hebrew language appear where the god's name might have been written. Transliterated to the English alphabet the letters would be "YHWH." Some have translated the letters to stand for the name Yahweh (some, earlier, translations of the text named the god, Jehovah). The deity is male, a bachelor, and one who seems to have no interest in sex (very different from the gods of Greece or India). He is characterized contrarily — that is, sometimes, he is fierce, sometimes, he is benevolent and caring. Moses, for example, is quoted as saying, "The Lord is a man of war." And, he says that to obey "YHWH," the people are to mercilessly slaughter their enemies, man, woman and child. Moreover, "YHWH" punishes to the third and fourth generations those who violate his laws. On the other hand, the prophets write about "YHWH" as one who is devoted to high moral principles of compassion, mercy and justice. The prophet, Amos, states that YHWH cares nothing for ceremonial rituals, directed toward him, but desires only that people practise justice. And Hosea, Micah and Isaiah make similar statements, affirming YHWH and his care for the whole human race (he is a "father" to orphans, and a "husband" to widows, it is said).

A second idea is that this god uses a book to communicate with people. That book was in a process of being written (and revised) until AD 90 or 100 when Jews decided by some official concensus that the book was complete. Whereas books are commonplace to the modern world, at that time, books were a rare technology in the communication business. So, what they had was impressive. They were the only people in the Mediterranean area, prior to Christianity, with a book that they could use to support their claims to being a special group of people. The book carried a sacred tradition back much further than the Roman Empire or the Greek Empire. And the book was not a secret book, written only for priests. The style was open, simple, plain. And the book recorded much that might not be, particularly, pious or praiseworthy — there is Noah's incest with his daughters and King David's adulteries.

A second book called *Talmud* stands alongside the scripture book and explains how the requirements of the covenant relationship are to be applied in specific situations. In short, it is a highly developed commentary and interpretation written over centuries. In many respects, it is a form of casuistry that argues from a legal principle taken from the scripture to specific cases encountered among ordinary people. And, in this sense, there are many areas for application: agricultural matters, marriage, family, divorce, rituals of purification, pollution problems. It seems that every aspect of a person's life is accounted for, including what foods are suitable to be eaten (*kosher*) and what foods are not. The rules are extensive and detailed: animals must be slaughtered correctly, certain foods must not be mixed together, and some foods are prohibited.

A third significant and somewhat troubling teaching is about what might be termed "the predicament of mankind." The story of the creation of the world includes a story of the so-called "Fall" of mankind. It is the story of the first man, Adam and his wife, Eve. The two live in a paradise provided by YWHW; they are innocent, happy and all their needs are met. They were told that they might eat fruit from any tree in the garden except the tree that is in the middle of the garden. That tree is the "Tree of knowledge of Good and Evil." From that tree, they were not to eat.

But, the tree serves as a temptation. Eventually, the story says, a serpent in the garden encouraged Eve to taste the fruit of the tree. Eve took fruit from the tree, ate it, and gave some to Adam. And he ate the fruit, also. Their god, then, put them out of the garden and set a guard to prevent them from returning to the paradise. The text says that they were sent away so that they could not eat from "the tree of life" and live forever.

It is a strange story. But it is troubling, too. And it is important to notice that the forbidden tree was named the *Tree of the knowledge of Good and Evil*. Temptation was the temptation to know (knowledge, of course, is power — to know is to be able to do; and to be able to do requires moral decision). Adam and Eve were created, morally innocent. But intellectual growth to knowledge puts them into the moral sphere. The story seems to say that knowledge throws mankind into the moral realm. Knowledge always forces a person to choose. And the dilemma is that to choose not to choose is still to choose. Once a person chooses knowledge that person must face the choices of morality. The story suggests that there is no escape for a person choosing knowledge.

Yet, another teaching embedded in the scripture is a theory of history. In short, it is that their god (the god of all humanity, they insist) has a plan for history, a purpose. And because of that plan and purpose, what takes place in the world is very important (this view differs from the Hindu or Buddhist notions that what happens in the world will be of little significance to the spiritually sophisticated).

But Jews insisted that human history is supposed to conform to a divine plan. And people are supposed to see to it that the divine plan is installed in the world. Particularly leaders, rulers, are obligated to direct and order people to live according to the high standards of YHWH's commandments. This meant, first, that life in this world is real, important and meaningful (escape, release from life in the world is not a religious option for Jews). Moreover, the message of the religion is a social and political message: human life is to be ordered and organized, according to the laws of YHWH.

Vivid illustrations of such a theme are found in the stories about the prophets. The role of the prophets was to remind people — especially leaders — of the covenant relationship and the social requirements of that relationship. There appear to be three distinct phases to the roles, played by prophets. The first mention of prophets in the texts suggests that there were groups of men who wandered, conducted some sort of worship, and, apparently, experienced an emotional relationship to their god. A second phase saw the emergence of individuals out of the groups. Men such as Elijah, Elisha and Nathan were associated with the groups, but emerged from them and claimed to be spokesmen for YHWH. A strong ethical concern marked their messages. Nathan confronted King David about his adulterous relationship with Bathsheba. The king had carried on an adulterous relationship with Bathsheba, while her husband was on the front lines, fighting one of the king's wars. When pregnancy threatened to disrupt the tryst, the king attempted a "cover up" by giving her husband Uriah, military leave (it must be made to look as though Uriah made his wife pregnant). But, in an expression of loyalty to military service, Uriah would not approach his wife. The king's response was to order Uriah into a battle where he was soon killed.

The "cover up" was successful until the prophet, Nathan, approached the king and publically declared that he was both an adulterer and a murderer. The prophet, speaking for YHWH, uncovered what had been carefully covered. The king had succumbed to a common human failing involving both sex and deceit. But to cover it with murder was to act unjustly. The role of the prophet was to show injustice, where it might occur.

A third phase of the prophet movement involved prophets who wrote books that became included in Jewish scripture. These writing-prophets extended the ethical theme of the individual prophets. Writing prophets such as Amos, Hosea, Joel, Jeremiah and Isaiah saw a considerable gap between rich and poor, the powerful and the weak. And with remarkable insight, they insisted that evil had become institutionalized. Something was wrong with society, they insisted. The laws allowed injustice to creep into the structure of the society. Evil, they insisted, is not simply a matter of individual conduct, individual actions. Evil was a part of the social structure of a society that let religion flourish while the poor suffered. The writing-prophets vigorously attacked a complacent but unjust society.

A final significant teaching is that of "the kingdom of god." Their god, the writers claimed, would establish his rule on earth. And even as Adam and Eve had lived in a paradise of peace and innocence, walking with god "in the cool of the evening," so might mankind return to paradise. Some writers note that Jerusalem will be the city where the rule of god is to be established. The phrase "the Day of the Lord" is used by writers as diverse as Isaiah and writers of "Psalms." To some Jews "the Day of the Lord" meant a triumph of Jews over enemies. To others, it meant that labour would end, peace would be established, and sickness and death eliminated. But some writers, such as the prophet Amos, insisted that the Day of the Lord would be a day of justice, where judgement against evil people would occur.

The rule of god, however, would be established through an agent of god who, it was said, would appear in the world. He was to be *messiah* ("anointed"). He would be identified as a descendant of King David. Jerusalem would be the initial place of his rule but he would extend his rule to the whole world. Various descriptions claim that he is to appear as a judge, as a saviour, as a peace-maker, as an opponent of all tyrants, and as one with abilities to turn nature into a paradise. In short, there is to be a return to the paradise experienced as the Garden of Eden.

15

The Rest of the Jewish Story

Jerusalem, the so-called "holy city," suffered a devastating attack by the Roman army in AD 70. A rebellion of Jews instigated the march of the Roman armies to Palestine. The attack resulted in the destruction of much of the city, including the temple for worship. And as punishment for rebellion against Rome, the Jewish people were forced out of the land (once again).

The "scattering" of the Jews is known to Jewish history as *The Diaspora* (The Great Dispersion). Jews "dispersed" north and south out of Palestine. Those who moved north into Europe became known as *Ashkenasim*. Those who moved south and across North Africa and even into Spain have been known as *Sefardim*.

It is important to remember that in the centuries following the "Dispersion," Christian religion came to dominate the societies of Europe. The Roman Emperor, Constantine, in the fourth century AD, declared himself to be a Christian; he provided imperial backing for the growing religion that, whose adherents insisted, they fulfilled Jewish religion, by identifying the Messiah. Jesus of Nazareth, they insisted, was the long-awaited anointed one. But Jews rejected that notion and, in fact, leaders of the faith had some complicity in the execution of Jesus.

The Jews in Christian Europe

The Christian triumph resulted in domination by the Church of all things social and political throughout most of Europe. Economic, political, social and intellectual life were influenced by the Christian teachings. Universities had a theological curriculum and faculty. The Cristian Pope and the so-called "Holy Roman Emperor" controlled political matters from Italy to England. In such a society, Jews were a distinct and identifiable minority group.

There was a double role for such a minority to play in Christian society. One was a theological role. And one was an economic role. The theological role was that Jews were the rejecters of Jesus. The very people, to whom god had sent the *messiah*, had rejected him. And they voiced no objection to his execution by Roman soldiers. In fact, the Jews were identified as "Christ killers."

Through the centuries, a vast number of Jews paid the price of death because of this attitude, often, explicitly stated by Christian leaders. Moreover, if Jews lived in misery, they deserved to live in misery, it was thought; they had consciously rejected Jesus as the long-awaited *messiah* (their lives of misery stood as visible witness to the future of any who neglected proper recognition of Jesus). Jews were theologically on the outside — and because they were theologically wrong, they were socially, culturally and politically on the outside, too.

The economic role was more positive. Although Jews were restricted from diversifying economic activities (many areas of employment were prohibited to Jews), the restrictions forced Jews into areas of "marginal legitimacy." What that meant was that Jews were forced into banking, money-lending, trade, economic speculation and investment. What made such areas "marginal" was that Christian teachings of the time regarded money-lending, with a charge of interest, to be "unnatural" and, therefore, sinful. To have money reproduce itself is to have money do something "unnatural" — money cannot by itself "reproduce." Money-lending, as a way to reproduce money, is as unnatural and sinful as homosexuality (Church teaching maintained that sex is legitimate so long as the sexual act might be to produce a child; but, the same sex cannot produce a child, thus, homosexual relations are unnatural — indeed, against nature — and, therefore, sinful).

But, Jews had no such "natural law" with restrictions placed upon them by their theology. And the economics of trade required investment, banking, money-lending and finance. So, by default, Jews were forced into areas which promised significant economic gain. The difficult social situation for Jews, who were forced to play this double role in society, is nicely illustrated in William Shakespeare's drama, *The Merchant of Venice*. Shylock, the Jew, is at once a symbol of evil, but, at the same time, the only one capable of providing money for people in difficult financial straits.

One way for Christian society to deal with the double role for Jews was the *ghetto*. The word means "restricted," and it was the place for Jews in nearly every European city. Usually, separated from Christian society by a wall as well as "Jewry laws" restricting their activities, ghettoes provided some advantages for Jewish society. Separation allowed Jews to develop their communities unhampered by Christian and/or secular laws and regulations. "Jewry laws" applied to them in their relations with the larger community of Christians. But Jews were free to develop laws to govern themselves in the ghetto. So, in some ways, religious life was enhanced by the opportunities to make

Torah central to life. Days of religious ceremony, clothing, food and customs were made a matter of Jewish identity. And a distinct theology put before the people reminders of the Promise to Abraham, the Covenant, and the Land. And, indeed, in some times and places, a call for a return under a *messiah* occurred.

But, along with advantages, there were also disadvantages to the ghetto. A major disadvantage, of course, was that everyone knew who the Jews were and where they lived. And a regular occurrence during the middle ages of Western culture were attacks upon the ghettoes. A particularly dangerous time for Jews were Christian celebrations. Easter season seemed a favourite time for Christians who might be eager to show their piety to loot and burn ghetto areas.

The Enlightenment Period and Change in Jewish Status

The period of European history, known as *Enlightenment*, thought to have begun sometime after the 1685 publication of Isaac Newton's book titled *Mathematical Principles of the Universe*, brought change to the status of Jews. The book, written by a pious Christian, opened the doors of Western intellectual life to the powerful persuasive forces of modern science. What Newton championed, possibly without knowing it, was a new epistemology, a new way of discovering knowledge about the world. The term "Enlightenment" has come to mark the growing optimism among intellectuals. And, in the heady world of the intellectuals, a great new and refreshing confidence about science and the future prevailed.

Enlightenment-thinkers had their own beliefs about the

world — beliefs which, often, ran counter to traditional religious beliefs. The universe, they insisted, is an orderly and rational collection of things whose relations are governed by natural laws. Moreover, human beings are capable of understanding such laws and using them to benefit mankind. To gain knowledge that counts, that matters, is not to be done by consulting the authorities of the past (neither the *Bible* nor the philosophers of antiquity). In fact, what is needed is a sustained questioning of traditional religious and philosophical ideas. And, such questioning will show that ancient thinkers had been wrong about many matters.

One interesting consequence of this way of thinking was a new tolerance and openness among many people in Western Europe. The scientific method of acquiring knowledge (at least, theoretically) does not care about who discoveres something. It bases conclusions upon demonstrable public testing. And hand in hand with the new tolerance came a new society. The democratic revolutions of Europe occurred while the intellectual revolution was taking place. In country after country, the nobility, the aristocracy, the kings, were pushed out of their positions of power and democratic states were organized. This occurred in England and France. And Americans (in theory, at least) had no patience for any who favoured either king or a ruling aristocracy.

One consequence of this thinking was that the ghetto, in many areas, became a thing of the past (Jews were even invited to participate in the cultural, social and political life of Europe and America).

None of this occurred immediately of course. And it did not occur without social struggle. But, slowly, it began to occur. In fact, in some places in America, Jews were encouraged to establish their own territories and to govern themselves.

But, again, there were both advantages and disadvantages. Jews were recognized as citizens with rights which were the same as or other citizens. They were allowed to vote in the democratic regimes. They were not restricted by law from diversifying their economic activities. In short, they were free to participate in democratic societies. And these were new and wonderful advantages.

Disadvantage that accompanied the new freedom had much to do with the fact that Jews now had to address the epistemological issues which science tends to raise for modern people, everywhere. In other words, "How do we know what we claim to know?" Could Jews rest their claims to the covenant promises simply by citing the their holy books? Many in the new environment of freedom (and science) thought that they could not merely cite a holy book to justify truth-claims. So Jews were forced to enter the intellectual culture of European and American life.

The Faith of Modern Jews

A movement advocating change occurred among some of the Jews of Germany in the mid-nineteenth century. Main thinkers were Zechariah Frankel and Abraham Geiger. These adopted what they called a "positive-historical" approach to Jewish history and its claims. In 1843 advocates of this approach published a statement, citing three fundamental principles: First, they insisted, the possibility of *unlimited development* must be affirmed (this, of course, over against traditional notions that *Torah* had a finality to it). Second, they insisted, *Talmud* possesses no authority from a doctrinal or a practical standpoint. The rituals and ceremonies and beliefs of *Talmud* are not required. And third, there need be neither expectation nor desire for a *messiah* to lead Jews back to Palestine. In short, there is no need for a special land (one's land of birth is sufficient).

Reform-Jews emphasized *social ethics* as the essence of the faith. They relied upon the statements of the prophets that had talked about justice and mercy in society. And they insisted that Jewish faith talked of the brotherhood of all mankind. And many Reform-Jews understood the faith to call them to social service in professions of law, medicine and teaching.

But many Jewish people could not tolerate the radical nature of the Reform Movement. To deny authority to *Torah* or *Talmud* on "positive-historical" grounds is a risky and foolish project. Where does one stop with such foolishness, they asked. What authority, then, does any tradition possess? And what happens to a culture made empty of tradition?

Conservative Judaism

Unhappy and unsettled with what many thought to be an abandonment of text and tradition, some Jews rallied to the ideas of a man named Solomon Schechter. Calling themselves Conservatives as against what was seen as the "radical" Reform Movement, these published eight principles which were thought to convince Jews to return to the tradition. Four of those principles are, particularly, relevant to the new attitudes toward change. First, they insisted, change is inevitable but not always unambiguously good. Some change might bring decay. Second, truth that stands as proven is not to be denied or ignored. In short, science and its methods must be affirmed, and where scientific conclusions are contrary to tradition or text, the issue must be addressed. However, the "truth" of the *Talmud* must be preserved as the basis for a way of life. Which is to say, fourthly, that Judaism is a way of life, not simply an ethical system. Judaism is a culture, a civilization, a tradition which is to shape the lives of people who are children of the Covenant system. It is a culture, a civilization, a tradition which shapes the whole of life (not just conduct in social affairs).

A third group are those Jews who choose to live closest to text and tradition. These are Orthodox Jews. There are varieties of Orthodox Jews having to do with geographic areas of East and West Europe. All, however, wish to consistently maintain beliefs and practices contained in *Torah* and spelled out in *Talmud*. The legal suysem of *Torah* must be maintained, these insist. Moreover, the ritual and ceremonial requirements of *Talmud* must be not only preserved, but practised. Orthodox Judaism holds the loyalties of the majority of Jews, possibly because the majority of Jews in the world lived in Eastern European countries such as Poland, Rumania, Russia and the old Ottoman Empire centred in Turkey. Jews of Eastern Europe knew the ghetto as a way of life well into the twentieth century. And, in the ghettoes of Eastern Europe, Jewish life remained very much like it had been for centuries. And, even when some Orthodox communities came to America, no significant change took place. In fact, a tenet of some Orthodox Jews is that life must continue the way it had been lived for centuries (this is the norm for Jews, they say — in spite of the fact that the norm is what was established in the middle ages, not Palestine). Identification, as Jewish life of the European ghetto, has meant to many that there is no point in participation in the economic and social life of any community which is not Jewish. To be a Jew is to be cut-off from the community of non-Jews. Jews are a separate and chosen people. And it might be added that Orthodox Jews abhor Reform and Conservative interpretations of the faith. To abandon Orthodoxy is to abandon Jewishness, to abandon the Covenant relationship. And in some cases, Orthodox Jews will hold a funeral service for family members who abandon the Orthodox way.

Zionism

The traditional sense of Zionism for Jews was a desire to return to the land believed to have been given by their god to Abraham. And when that return is made by a significant number of Jews, the *messiah* will appear and establish the rule of the Jewish god on earth.

But a new Zionism has appeared, in recent history. The new Zionism is political, militant, non-religious. This new Zionism has had three different expressions. In 1896 Theodore Herzl published a book, titled *The Jewish State.* In the book, Herzl argued that Jews must have a homeland to shield them from oppression they faced in Europe and America. And for Herzl, it did not matter where the state would be established (he considered parts of Africa). The argument was, that, since no one else wanted Jews as countrymen, let them have a state, a political entity of their own. Herzl insisted on political status. Since this could and would shield the religion.

Orthodox and Reform Jews opposed Herzl's Zionism. Reform-Jews insisted that the religion is strictly religion and that it need have no political status. In fact, to talk about a state is to confuse religion and politics, to the detriment of religion. Orthodox Jews didn't like the message of Herzl, either. The Orthodox view was that a move to Palestine must be initiated by their god through a *messiah*. And Herzl, something of a dandy in Vienna cafe society, surely, was no *messiah*. Moreover, Herzl's talk might create more persecution, since talk of loyalty to an Israeli state will raise questions of Jewish patriotism for Jews in any other country. So much for Herzl's "Political Zionism."

A different sort of Zionist talk appeared with the publication of *Selected Essays* in 1912, written by Ashor Ginsberg (known, later, as Achad Haam). Ginsberg was concerned that Jewish spiritual life was disintegrating because of the influences of Christianity and Islam. Thus, a homeland for Jews to develop the historic faith and culture is necessary, he insisted. An elite group of Jews from all over the world should gather in one place to recover and develop the faith. A state — political sovereignty and organization — is not necessary, he maintained. A famous name, associated with this "Cultural Zionism," is that of the philosopher, Martin Buber.

A third Zionist movement is that known as "Radical Zionism." Advocated by a man, named Herman Cohen, in his publication *The Reconstructionist*, this movement makes a distinction between *nationality* and *nationhood*. Jews are not simply a religious community, Cohen argues. They are a nationality. A nationality is a biological and historical unity, whereas nationhood refers to a political unity only. It is important that Jews preserve their nationality. But, Cohen insists, nationality can be preserved within the framework of already existing nations. The essence of Jewish nationality is *messianic*. That is, Jews are a living example of the unity of mankind. There are Jews of every nationality, every race. They cannot be confined to one local, separate state.

Debates among Jews about Zionism continued until Adolph Hitler in the 1930s rose to power in Germany and began an effort to eliminate Jews from European societies. Before the rise of Hitler, however, the British government established the Balfour Declaration (1917), allowing Jews to return to territory the British controlled in Palestine. During the 1920s, Jewish immigration to Palestine had increased, steadily, money was raised, and the Jewish Agency was established to organize immigration efforts. Britain abandoned the Balfour Declaration in 1939, because of pressure from Arab states in the region as well as from Palestinian people, who were often displaced by Jews who entered the land. Jews, however, continued to enter and tensions between Arabs and Jews continued. The United Nations Special Committee on Palestine recom-mended partition of Palestine into a Jewish state and a state for the Palestinian people in 1947. But, in 1948, the British left the area. Jews declared the State of Israel. Arabs, who supported the Palestinian people, attacked. A war was fought and an armistice was reached in 1949. However, Jews won diplomatic recognition for the new state of Israel from the major world powers shortly later.

The views of many of the Arabs (and the Palestinian people's view) is that Jews made a lawless invasion of private territory and property. Many Palestinians were forced from their homes and businesses by Jews. Fighting forced additional hundreds of thousands to leave homes. Refugee camps numbered up to 900,000 Palestinians, displaced and without homes or occupations.

The nation of Israel favours an Orthodox Judaism as an established faith of the land. Orthodox Jews regard the existence of the nation as the fulfilment of the covenant-promise to Abraham. The United Nations continues to arbitrate disputes between Palestinians and Jews. The general view is that there should be a Palestinian state, established by asking Israel to give back the land taken from Palestinians.

So today there is a peculiar situation with regard to Israel. Inconsistencies — indeed, contradictions — abound. Herzl's view of *Political Zionism* has triumphed (but it is supported and sustained by Orthodox Jews — those that, in the past, had opposed him, vigorously). Jews (a people with forefront movements, calling for principles of a free, open society), in Israel hold to a system that is closed to participation by non-Jews. Zionism began and won support as a movement to end the *diaspora* and to find a homeland for Jews. Yet, today the nation of Israel is dependent upon Jews, living in Europe and America, for its survival. Moreover, Zionism was supported by many because Jews needed a place to be safe. Yet, Israel is not a safe place for Jews. Nearly every month, there are new and frightening terrorist attacks against Jews in Israel. Zionism brought Jews back to the land of the Covenant, but it has not been a convincing success in establishing the rule of the Jewish god. Some people have argued that Zionism, in that sense, has been a failure.

16

The Christian Religion

THE study of Christian religion and its origins begins with a problem: Christianity is a religion concerned with history, but the historical events concerning the life of the man, thought to be its founder, are difficult to determine. The major source for information is the Christian scripture, the *New Testament.* This book, which Christians add to the Hebrew scripture, is a collection of documents which include accounts of the life and teachings of Jesus Christ (the Gospels), a brief history of some early Christians (the "Acts of the Apostles"), and a variety of letters (epistles), written to Christians living in various parts of the Roman Empire. A fundamental argument, sometimes explicitly stated and other times assumed, is that Jesus of Nazareth (named the *Christ* — "anointed") brought to fulfilment the covenant-promises. Many stories about Jesus are used to substantiate this claim that Jesus was the long-expected *messiah.*

References in the text indicate that Jesus was born during the reign of the Roman emperor Augustus (Caesar Augustus). He died during the reign of Tiberius Caesar. He lived for a time as a carpenter in Nazareth (North Palestine). And, then, he served as an itinerant preacher and teacher, travelling through most of Palestine.

As a teacher and preacher, he irritated the Jewish

religious authorities. And, he violated some of the rules of proper Jewish conduct — for example, he associated with those thoughts to be sinners, and he did not obey all of the rules regarding the holy day of the week, the *sabbath*.

Eventually, Jesus was put to death by the Roman government rulers of Palestine under the charge of conspiracy to overthrow the government (together with the change of blasphemy levelled at him by the Jewish authorities). However, given the gospel accounts, it is difficult to see how a charge of either conspiracy or blasphemy might be substantiated. And, this fact leads many historians to be troubled by what must be regarded as a lack of specific data about the man himself and about his life and death.

The Teaching of Jesus

The Gospel, according to St. Mark, carries a summary statement of Jesus teaching. The text says, "Now, when John, the Baptist, had been put into prison, Jesus came into Galilee, preaching: 'The time is fulfilled, and the kingdom of God is at hand: repent, ye, and believe the gospel.' " This extremely concise statement might be a puzzle to anyone living in a culture, quite different, from Jewish culture of the first century AD. What is the significance of this call to repent and to believe?

A key word in the statement is *repent*. The text, passed along to the modern reader, is written in Greek, the *koine* Greek, or vernacular Greek, used in the Mediterranean region by many people. The word translated as "repent" is *metanoia*, and it is a strong word-meaning much more than the English words to have "sorrow," "regret" or "contrition." The Greek word means to, *to turn around, to do an about-face*. It is as if a person were intending to travel to the south pole, but were to start his journey by travelling north. To arrive at his intended destination, it would be wise for him to do *metanoia*.

It is important to remember that Jesus said this to proper, law-abiding, religiously respectable people, who practised considerable discipline in keeping themselves pure and spotless before their god. In short, he said to them that they were wasting their time to work at their public performance of religion because they were headed in the wrong direction. So, it appears that Jesus was criticising Jewish religion as it was being practised not only by ordinary people but by the leaders, too. In fact, in some parts of the *St. Matthew Gospel* and the *St. Luke Gospel*, he even suggests that of all the world's bad people, religious people are capable of being the worst.

A second important part of his teaching is his announcement that "The kingdom of god is at hand." There is no doubt that some of his hearers took this message to mean that God was about to establish Israel as an *independent state* through which he would start his rule on earth (that is, some thought the covenant-promise to Abraham, Isaac, and Jacob was to be fulfilled).

Through the centuries, however, Christians have held views differing from the Jewish convenant-promise view concerning the kingdom of god (most Christians, through the centuries, have been gentiles, not Jews, so they could not interpret the covenant-promises literally). So, some Christians have insisted that Jesus was talking about the kingdom of heaven, that is, his words should be interpreted as talk about life after death.

Others have understood the "kingdom" of god to mean the rule of god in the world, involving the moral reorganization of life according to Jesus' teachings. This interpretation puts much emphasis upon Jesus' words about peace, non-violence and generosity: "love your neighbour as yourself," "turn the other cheek if a man strikes you on one cheek," "give a man, who has need of your shirt, your coat also."

Yet, another interpretation of the talk about a kingdom is that Jesus was saying that something significant was about to happen through the work of god. And these Christians insist that it is the work of god, not of people to reorganize things. A good Christian should repent and wait for god to act, these interpreters insist.

A reasonable historical interpretation ties Jesus' teaching of the kingdom to the messianic expections that Jews held at that time (that is, authoritative Jews had written about and encouraged expectations of a *messiah* to bring about the rule of God in the world). That is to say that a credible interpretation must be tied to, connected to the expectations of people living, at that time.

A third important element in the teaching of Jesus is the moral context in which he talked about repentence and the kingdom. He addressed his message to people who, he said, needed to repent, to turn around with respect to their behaviour. The consequences of repentance would be to show a sensitivity to people with particular needs: give to others your shirt and your coat if they need them; go with a person a second mile if he or she asks you to accompany them one mile; love your enemies and pray for people that do bad things to you; to make peace is far better than making preparation for war; and he insisted that all of these things, their god does for them and for all mankind. So, to live the way he taught, would be to live according to the standards held by the god of Abraham, Isaac, and Jacob — the god of the covenant.

Problems Christians Encountered with the Teaching

From the earliest years and on, through the centuries, Christians have had difficulties with the teachings of Jesus. There are two major reasons for this. The first might be thought of as a theoretical problem. In short, Jesus put his message into an apocalyptic context: the world, as it was known, was going to come to an end. Matthew's Gospel, Mark's Gospel, and Luke's Gospel give accounts of Jesus' talk of the end of the world. One account maintains that some people present would not see death until all of the apocalyptic events spoken of would occur.

But, the world did not come to an end. And this was a problem to the earliest Christians (some of whom waited, in Jerusalem for the final end of things). And it has remained a puzzle for centuries, eliciting from Christians, responses ranging from stony silence to announcements that the end of the world would occur soon. That is, some Christians do not talk about this problem, while others insist that the end is near.

But a question remains. Does this apparent mistake cancel the teaching of Jesus? If he was wrong about the end of the world, does that mean he was wrong about loving one's neighbour, turning the other cheek, making peace? Christians have, vigorously, pointed to the logical fallacy in suggesting that it cancels the teaching: the origin of an idea has nothing to do with its validity. To think that his error about the end of the world means he was also wrong about morality is to commit what is known, in logic, as the genetic fallacy. Talk about the end of the world, however, did add an intensity to the teachings of Jesus.

But, Christians encountered a practical problem as well: How is it possible to put the teachings into practice? And, Jesus himself, when instructing people to love their neighbour, was asked, "Who is my neighbour?" Jesus answered that question with the story about The Good Samaritan. That man helped a "someone," he encountered, who had been robbed and beaten. The answer, the story gives, is that anyone in need of assistance that a person encounters is a neighbour. But, how might anyone apply that rule to ordinary life? And, what might it mean to try to apply that moral rule? It might mean followers of the teachings should support public welfare programmes to provide for the basic needs of all people. Or, how is a person to apply the rule "Resist not evil" or the rule "Blessed are the peacemakers?" Are Christians to oppose the military, everywhere? Is a moral obligation to be felt towards the *needs* of people or towards the *rights* of people. Western legal systems strongly favour rights of people against the needs of people.

Limitations

Many things about Jesus, no one knows. Although the four Gospels of Christian scriptures tell stories about Jesus, there is little information about the man himself. For example, there is no physical description given. There is no account of his formative years as a youth and young adult. In fact, there is very little personal information about him.

His teachings were similar to that of the prophets of the Jewish scripture. He showed little interest in the external or ceremonial aspects of Jewish religion. But he was very much interested in the inward aspects of the religion (for example, what is on the mind of a person when he or she prays?). Jesus seemed to be free of the prejudices many Jews had, towards non-Jews. He emphasized a universalism which seemed to run counter to the popular view that Jews were, especially, "chosen."

Jesus' message about "forgiveness" is important. He insisted that god forgives sinners. And, even when suffering the brutal and painful crucifixion, the text claims that, he said, "Father, forgiven them, for they do not know what they do!"

Moreover, Jesus did not seem to think of himself as the author of a new religion: he spoke in terms of Jewish faith all the time. And, he made no explicit general claim to be divine (that is, he did not ask people to recognize him as divine). He seemed to regard himself as the *messiah,* however. But, he did not try to convince people by the argument that he had the proper ancestry. And he did not talk about dying so that people might be forgiven of their sins (he taught rather that repentance and proper living was the key to entering the Kingdom of God). Nor did he baptize or prescribe baptism as necessary.

He did criticise the formalism of the Jewish priests and called them blind guides. And, he shared the popular superstitions of the times: texts say he did exorcisms and that he worked miracles. And, he said that when the world came to an end, sinners would be put into a furnace of fire.

The End of Jesus' Life

Jesus angered both the Jewish religious establishment people and the Roman authorities. He was arrested, tried and condemned to death as a subversive — that is, he was subverting the rule of Rome. The specific charges against Jesus — that he was a revolutionary and that he did not owe proper allegiance to the Roman emperor — are difficult to assess. It seems that the Jewish authorities, supported this allegation more as a means to get rid of him than as a serious charge which mattered to them.

What Jesus taught gained great significance, however, because his followers became convinced that he did not remain dead. The followers of Jesus claimed that Jesus came back from the dead, that he was resurrected from the dead. Many people have a great deal of trouble accepting as true, this claim. People who are dead don't get up and walk around and talk. Yet, the followers of Jesus became convinced that Jesus did. The fact that they were convinced cannot be disputed (why they were convinced, evidence for their conviction, is another question). Peter was the first to be convinced. All the followers, eventually, shared this conviction. It was the turning point in the conversion of Saul (known to later Christians as St. Paul). And the resurrection teaching played a central role in providing the courage for the early missionary efforts.

The conviction about the resurrection was deepened by the experience known as *Pentecost*. Jews had long celebrated a holiday known as Pentecost (fifty weeks after the beginnings of the Passover celebration). The so-called "Day of Pentecost" is noted among Christians as the day the spirit of the god of the Jews descended upon the closest followers of Jesus (known as "the disciples" or, later, "apostles"). These men had gathered in Jerusalem after the crucifixion. The scripture text, titled *The Acts of the Apostles*, says that they received a "baptism in the Holy Ghost." The visible consequence of the experience was that they began to speak spontaneously in languages that they had not known previously. But, Jews from other parts of the empire who were in Jerusalem for the ceremonies, understood them to be saying things in languages of their regions. One thing that this experience meant to some followers, was that they were supposed to tell the Jesus' message to people of every language.

The meaning and significance of the Pentecostal experience has been controversial. Questions abound: Does, knowing about Jesus, give people some special gift for languages? Is a special experience required for the imparting of this ability? What is the significance of this experience to people living two thousand years later?

The Teaching of the Early Christians

The early Christians (followers of Jesus) talked about Jesus with great intensity and courage in the territories occupied by the Roman armies. Two important concepts dominate their talk and the writings. The concepts are based upon two words in the *koine* Greek spoken and written in the Mediterranean regions. The two words are *kairos* (time) and *kerygma* (proclamation).

The Greek language has two words for "time." One word is *chronos,* the base for the English word "chronological." *Chronos*-time is the sort of time measured by seconds, minutes, hours, days, weeks, months and years. Each segment is the same length (an hour is measured by sixty minutes, a full day by twenty-four hours, etc.). *Chronos*-time is *measurable time. Kairos*-time, however, is translated in the Christian scripture as "fulfilled time," "accepted time," indeed, "significant time." It implies that chronological time, divisible, measureable time has a dimension to it, not always recognized. Chronological time might be interrupted by *kairos* time. For example, a student might attend a class, day after day, to listen to lectures by a professor. But, then, the professor announces that there will be an examination. At that time, *chronos*-time becomes *kairos*-time. A student must put together all of the *chronos*-time into one *kairos*-time. Class time is "fulfilled," the significance of *chronos* has been reached, and its importance is being recognized by the examination. A student is expected to produce a proper response to the *kairos*.

What is important about *kairos* is that all previous time becomes suddenly significant, meaningful. The early Christians insisted that the time in which they lived was the *kairos*. Jesus, they said, had ushered in a new age. Time was fulfilled; the proper response to hearing about this was to repent and to believe. All people, they insisted, stood at crossroads of history. People, especially Jews, of course, need to decide. An intensity to the message was gained by such an interpretation of time.

A second major aspect of the early Christian religion was *kerygma*, "proclamation." The early Christians made a serious — even controversial — announcement, first, to Jews and, then, to Gentiles. The text, "The Acts of the Apostles," contains a number of such announcements. Seven ideas are clear from the different accounts. They maintained that it was the Jewish god who was acting through the life of Jesus (i.e., Jesus was the anointed one, the Christ, the *messiah*). Secondly, although crucified, Jesus was raised from the dead by the god. And third, this was done in order to keep the covenant promise, given to Abraham, Isaac and Jacob. Fourth, this meant that the covenant promise was fulfilled (a difficult claim for many Jews to accept, since the territory was ruled by Roman government). The means by which the covenant promise was fulfilled was by Jesus' death and resurrection. Jesus, therefore, is the lord (the king, the supreme ruler), they said. And this king, this heavenly ruler, will return to the earth to judge the living and the dead. The time between the event of Jesus' death and resurrection and the final consummation of all things is the decisive time, the *kairos*.

It must be noted that the message could make sense to Jews — that is, the early proclamation ties the significance of Jesus to the history of Jewish religion (the covenant agreement with Abraham, Isaac, Jacob, etc.). It took a few years for the proclamation to be made relevant to non-Jews. A man, Saul of Tarsus (re-named Paul), universalized the message with a new, significant, and controversial theology which explained, further, the significance of Jesus.

Paul was an important Jewish rabbi, who initially opposed the Christians. But, then, he converted to the faith. He claimed that he had a visitation from the risen Jesus, while on a journey to confront and, possibly, arrest a group of Christians. After his conversion, he travelled throughout the Mediterranean region teaching about Jesus. His letters to various church groups make up a significant part of *The New Testament* (the "new covenant").

Paul was distinct from some of the Christians because he insisted that the Christian-teaching should be proclaimed to everyone, Jews and non-Jews. His technique of teaching was to approach, first, a synagogue and proclaim the message there. Usually, he was thrown out. Then, he proclaimed the message to non-Jews, many of whom welcomed him into their homes. He managed to establish congregations of Christians all over the Roman empire regions.

Justification by Faith

Paul's message was simple and inclusive. It might be summed up in his phrase stated in his "Letter to the

Romans," claiming *justification is by faith in Jesus, the Christ.* All people are separated from God because of Adam's sin, he said. And sin is, therefore, a *condition*, not only certain actions or deeds. Sin is the condition of being separated from the Jewish god, who is the one God of all mankind. The Tenth Commandment, handed down through Moses, proves that all people are separated from God, he insisted. The Commandment says, "Thou shalt not covet thy neighbour's wife, nor his manservant, nor his maidservant, nor his ox, nor his ass, nor anything that is thy neighbour's." That is to say, a person should not even *want* something that belongs to someone else. Sin is a condition in which people *want* and *desire* things that belong to others.

But, Paul maintained, all people are now reconciled to God because of Jesus, the Christ, the anointed one, the *messiah*: "As in Adam, all died, so, in Christ, all are made alive," he insisted. The first man, Adam, disobeyed and he was banished from paradise. But Christ has brought forgiveness and reconciliation. The decisive factor is faith, trust: "The just shall live by faith," Paul wrote.

This interpretation of Jewish history and the Jesus story had great appeal to the Gentile population of the Empire. Paul added an additional factor: he identified Jesus with the God of the whole world. It is important to remember that Paul talked to and wrote to Gentiles, non-Jews. These people were not looking for a *messiah*. These people knew nothing of the Covenant. So Paul explained the meaning of Jesus to these people by saying that he was God, appearing as a man. Christ, he wrote, was the divine being, who possessed the nature of god, but, who had humbled himself, had entered the world as a human being, had suffered death by crucifixion and had been raised from the dead, so that he could demonstrate his victory over death. Now, Paul wrote, Jesus sits on the throne off God (at the right hand of God) and he will return to judge the world.

Paul captured the minds of thousands of people with such a message. No doubt groundwork for this sort of talk had been laid by what are known to historians of religion as *The Mysteries*, groups of devotees to Dionysus. Hermes, Isis, Osiris, Mithraism, Diana. The mysteries all taught about a divine being who entered the world as a saviour, a saviour who could give immortality to people who became followers. Generally, a conversion experience was encouraged. And, conversion required the abandonment of one way of living in favour of a new life and new companions. Often, the new way of life involved a new moral stance, in some cases, advocating non-violence and brotherly love. Paul made much of the new way of living that the Christian teaching advocated. And his letters to various groups living in sometimes hostile environments encouraged forgiveness and love.

So, Christians proclaimed that there is but one God. And God revealed himself in the life, death and resurrection of Jesus. The purspose of the Jesus event was to restore a broken relationship between God and all of mankind. Paul's famous statement summing up the message was "God was in Christ, reconciling the world to Himself."

17

Finding Good Reasons for Believing

Cultivated people of the Roman Empire who encountered the Christian teaching in the first century thought it to be somewhat vulgar (Christian teaching was another of the "mystery" cults, many Romans assumed, because it talked about bodies, blood, spirits and immortality). The Roman writer Tacitus referred to Christianity as "a pernicious superstition." Seutonius agreed. And Pliny, after investigating the religion, concluded that Christians were not, in fact, monsters, but they did believe what he called "a depraved and extravagant superstition."

Yet, the Christian teaching became established in the Mediterranean regions. It survived and grew at the same time as the mystery teachings about Mithra, Isis, Ankh, Osiris, and Dionysus disappeared.

Christianity survived and grew by creating an impressive and convincing theology that combined Jewish talk about a *messiah* with categories of Greek philosophy. This remarkable achievement did not take place without a struggle, however. Many Christians of that time (as well as today) insisted that faith need not be rational. An influential Christian theologian of that time, Tertullian, maintained that "I believe because it is absurd." Yet, other Christians insisted that the teaching must make rational sense or it was of no value. And these Christians constructed an impressive theology by synthesizing Christian claims with Greek philosophy.

Apologists

Apologist is a name given to a number of men who had been educated as philosophers in the schools of Alexandria, Egypt, or Athens, Greece. At some point in their lives, these men became Christians; they, then, took upon themselves the task of defending Christian teaching, when and where it was attacked by sophisticated critics. The word *Apology* in the Greek language means "defence." An Apologist is a "defender." Some famous defenders were Justin the Martyr, Clement of Alexandria, Cyprian, Origen and Ireneus.

The arguments against Xnty were many. A summary of the arguments is provided by Celsus in his book, *True Discourse* (AD 177). Celsus was a philosopher of Neo-Platonic persuasion. His arguments against Christianity were four. First, he argued, Christianity rests upon claims that Jesus was resurrected from the dead. This claim is questionable on two counts, he insisted. Only believers in Jesus were witnesses, who could testify that they saw him (and most of these were hysterical women). And second, claims about resurrections are ordinary claims: nearly every emperor, countless military heroes, and others have been seen after they died (it had been claimed).

Moreover, the teaching that God entered the world as Jesus of Nazareth is irrational and subversive. The best arguments for the existence of God that Greek philosophy provides conclude that God, to be God, must be unchangeable, self-sufficient, in need of nothing. But claims that God changed and entered the world as an infant, born in Palestine, subvert the arguments for the existence of God.

And even if it were to happen, to suppose it would happen to the Jews (of all people) makes no rational sense. If God could and would do such a thing, it would make sense for him to visit Athens or Alexandria, where he could confront critical minds. And to insist that God did this act only once, doesn't make sense either (if he were to do it, surely, he would do it every now and again so that a lot of people would know about it). And claims that Jewish scripture told ahead of time about Jesus' life are a manipulation of words (it is to interpret badly the Jewish scripture). For example, no kingdom of God has come out of Palestine (in fact, the Roman armies put down a revolt of Jews, destroyed the temple, and chased the Jews out of the area). And lastly, Christianity is a political threat (the Roman government has established peace all over the Mediterranean region: for Christians to claim that the kingdom of God has been established is to give allegiance to a foreign power).

Apologist Response to Criticism

The Apologists, in their response to critics, such as, Celsus, did not engage in arguments about history or about government. Instead, they appealed to reason in an effort to show that the Christian teaching fulfilled Greek philosophy. Whereas Jewish Christians had argued that Christian teaching fulfilled Hebrew thought, Apologists claimed that Christian teaching fulfilled Greek philosophy. Justin, the Martyr, said that wherever truth appears it is Christian truth: "What anybody has said about truth belongs to us." In short, Christianity embraces all truth (the Christians might not know all that is true, but Christianity accepts all that is true). And, anyone who ever lived according to what is true, is a Christian (this risky argument might force the conclusion that Socrates, Plato, and Aristotle, among others, were Christians without knowing that they were). One clarifying claim Apologists did make was that the appearance of Jesus in space and time meant that it is possible for even uneducated people to receive truth (formerly only smart, educated people could understand, but now the truth was lived and seen by ordinary people).

Apologists' View of God

The Apologists accepted a Greek philosophical view of God as an eternal being, impersonal, unchanging, an unmoved mover, that created the world. It is difficult to reconcile this view of God with the Jewish YHWH, who seemed to be terribly interested in rather mundane matters about what sort of food people ate, when and with whom they might engage in sexual relations, even what sort of clothes people should wear. That is to say, the laws and requirements written in the Hebrew texts *Deuteronomy* and *Leviticus* portray a divine busy body. But the Apologists ignored what might seem to be difficulties of reconciling the Greek philosophical notion of God and the Hebrew talk about YHWH.

A remarkable contribution of the Apologists was their interpretation of Jesus. Greek philosophers had insisted that there is a rational order to the universe. That is to say, the laws of reason hold everywhere (for example, it cannot be sensibly stated that a thing both exists and does not exist, at the same time: it cannot be sensibly stated that the same surface is both green and white at the same time). The orderliness of the world shows that there is a principle of order, that exists (the world has a rational structure that underlies it). And rational truths are truths that hold as the case, everywhere. Two plus two equals four in America, in China, in India, and on the moon. Moreover, the principle of "rational contradiction" exists, everywhere (something or someone cannot both exist and not exist, someone cannot both be in a particular place and not in that particular place).

Greek philosophers had named the rational ordering principle as *Logos*. Any mind encounters *Logos* when the truths of mathematics, geometry, logic are encountered and understood. The brilliant move of the Apologist thinkers was to take the idea of *Logos* from Greek philosophy and to identify *Logos* with Jesus. John's *Gospel* suggested this in the opening lines: "In the beginning was the *Logos* (translated in the King James translation as "Word") and the *Logos* was with God, the same was in the beginning with God." The Apologists insisted that the principle by which the absolute, unmoveable, unchangeable God shows himself to human beings is *Logos*. God revealed himself as reason, as rationality, as order in a world of human chaos and disorder. Human beings are prone to disorder and irrationality. But rational structure, order, has been revealed to mankind through *Logos*. The Christian Apologists asserted that the *Logos* had entered the world as Jesus of Nazareth.

The remarkable intellectual move made Christianity meaningful to the people of the Mediterranean region. The Apologists were saying, in effect, that the Christian teaching fulfilled Greek thought, too. And to argue the case for Christianity, a person did not need history (Hebrew scripture claims were irrelevant). What a person needed to become convinced of the claims of Christianity was a mind honed and sharpened by Greek philosophical logic. So, the

Apologists made a starting claim: Jesus was Reason in a human body.

But a consequence of this teaching was controversy. Inevitably, the question was asked about how could it be that *Logos* would take human form. How could the principle of reason enter a woman's uterus, become an infant, grow to adulthood (indeed, live the messy, inevitably disordered life in a Roman occupied territory), and continue to be *Logos*?

Two of the major teachings, officially, named as heresies emerged from such questions. Some Christians began to argue that God did not really become a human being. He simply made himself to appear as if he were human (the Greek verb "appear" is *dokeo*). The teaching, eventually, was known as *Docetism*. And Christian authorities declared it to be a false teaching, a heresy.

A second teaching that emerged from the difficulties presented by Greek philosophy was known as Arianism. This teaching (espoused by a man named Arius) insisted that Jesus was a man, but he was not divine. Jesus was a human being, empowered by God in a special way. Some wanted to insist that God "adopted" him at his baptism. Matthew's *Gospel* says that when Jesus arose out of the baptism water, "The heavens opened . . . and, lo, a voice from heaven, saying, "This is my beloved Son, with whom I am well pleased."

The result of controversies about Jesus was the famous Nicene Creed, a declaration, recited by Christians in worship services until this day. The Creed (originally written in Greek) states:

I believe in one God the Father Almighty, maker of

> heaven and earth: and in one Lord Jesus Christ, the only begotten of God, God of God, Light of Light, very God of very God, begotten, not made, being of one substance with the Father, by whom all things were made. . . .

The important lines are "God of God, Light of Light, very God of very God, begotten not made, being of one substance with the Father." The controversy among Christian thinkers was with the phrase "of one substance." The Greek word for "one substance" is *homoousios*. It is very similar to the Greek word for "similar substance," *homoiousious*. Yet, those who maintained, Jesus was of "similar" substance to God, were identified as heretics, false teachers. And, they were sent from the established (more populous and powerful) Church to establish themselves in their own places. These are regarded as the Eastern Church. So Christians, by the fourth century AD, were divided into Eastern and Western branches.

But, for both branches, East and West, Christian teaching had been made reasonable by putting together Hebrew teaching about a *messiah* with Greek philosophy. And many advocates of Christian teachings today insist upon "the reasonableness of Christianity." By combining Greek philosophy with Christian claims, the Christians of the Western world emerged as the intellectual winners among the competing cults of the time.

This is not to say that Christian thinkers were completely free from problematic questions. In fact, the solution to one problem created others. One question that troubled some thinkers was the question of *why Jesus had to do what he did*. Why did Jesus have to die a despicable and cruel death by crucifixion? And, if Jesus was *Logos* (Reason itself), why is there no record of him saying something that a Greek philosopher might find important?

Most troubling to many was the question of why it was necessary that Jesus died. And it took the Christian Church until the late eleventh century to find a suitable answer. And the answer was called *The Satisfaction Theory of Atonement*. In short, the theory (answer) maintains that the death of Jesus at the hands of the Roman governor of Palestine was reasonable and necessary. And the answer was constructed by a theologian and philosopher named Anselm of Canterbury (living from AD 1033-1109, a long distance from Palestine).

The problem arose because after the identification of Jesus as *Logos*, a particular way of thinking about the Christian claims as well as a particular way of thinking about Jesus was required. What this particular way of thinking demanded was rigorous rationality. Jesus wasn't just wandering around and carrying on casual conversations there in Palestine (for everything he did there had to be good reasons — logical reasons). Jesus had been identified with logic itself: and that meant that if he had been faced with alternative courses of action, he would have chosen the most reasonable alternative. Jesus as *Logos* would be reasonable, logical in word and deed.

But Jesus did not really add much to knowledge about God as the Greeks thought of God. And he did not even approach pressing philosophical problems such as how a perfect God could make an imperfect world or how if God is all-powerful and good and interested in people why it is that he could allow evil to exist.

More troubling for Anselm, however, was the question of why Jesus' activity in the world was so cumbersome and difficult (Jesus did not live an easy life or die an easy death). The confession of the earliest Christians was that Jesus entered the world to do something extremely important: "Christ died for our sins, " was the claim. What that might mean was answered by St. Paul in his letter to Roman Christians: Jesus died in order to reconcile humanity to God. But the new question was why Jesus needed to go through the difficult life he was made to live (according to the biblical accounts, birth in a stable, a difficult life of poverty, abuse by Jews and Romans, death by crucifixion). Why could God not simply forgive human beings? And, why was crucifixion necessary? Why did Jesus have to die in order for people to be reconciled to God?

Anselm's answer to such questions was that Jesus was bringing "satisfaction" to some requirement by dying the way he did. In short, Jesus was paying a debt. In his short book, titled, *Cur Deus Homo* (Why God Became a Man), Anselm argued that God could not forgive human sin, outright, because there are certain rational standards by which God must act. Sin is a debt, according to Anselm. And the problem that needs to be solved is that humanity needs to pay God so that the account can be settled, satisfied.

The puzzling thing to figure out is why do humans owe a debt to God, Anselm understood the situation in terms of the social situation of his time — the feudal society. Society, as he experienced it, was made up of a hierarchy of relationships. And what that meant for Anselm was that the seriousness of an offence was to be measured by the status of the person offended. An offence against a nobleman or a king was far more serious than an offence against a peasant. In short, kings and peasants do not relate to one another on a reciprocal basis: kings are far more important than peasants.

Because God created the world, he has higher status, higher rank, than any human being. Moreover, since God created the world and the people in it, all the world owes God for its very existence. Everyone owes God complete obedience, complete loyalty, complete devotion.

But no person has fulfilled this obligation to God. And that means that human beings owe something to God. But since human beings owe God everything anyway, there is simply no way to make up for the debt that has incurred by any lack of obedience, loyalty, devotion. The human predicament is that human beings owe to God what they cannot possibly pay to God because they cannot make up for past failures, the past debt. Human beings owe to God a debt which they cannot possibly pay. And God cannot and will not ignore such a fact. Nor can God simply cancel the debt (that would be contrary to the rational order of the universe).

The only solution to such a problem is a *god/man*: only God could pay the debt human beings owe to God. And that is why God became a man as Jesus (*cur deus homo*). In order to resolve the human predicament in a rational manner, God had to enter the world as a man so that he could live the perfect life and restore humanity to a proper relationship with God.

This Satisfication Theory of why God entered the world as a human being is basic to Christian theology. Jesus, it is said, entered the world as the God/man. And when he lived the perfect life that he did and died as he did, he satisfied the debt on behalf of all humanity. The Christian Church provides access to the benefits of satisfaction. Jesus said to Peter, according to Matthew's Gospel: "Thou art Peter, and upon this rock, I will build my church and the gates of hell, shall not prevail against it. Unto you I give the keys to the kingdom of God. Whatsoever you shall bind on earth will be bound in heaven. Whatsoever you shall loose on earth will be loosened in heaven."

A person's access to payment of the debt is through the Church, it is said. In the ritual of the Eucharist (among Roman Catholic Christians). Jesus is, once, again offered to God as a sacrifical payment. Those who participate in the ceremony receive the benefit of payment for sin.

This may seem to be an commercial approach to religion. But it remains a basic metaphor for Christian faith. Roman Catholic Christians continue, to this day, to re-enact the death of Jesus as payment for their debt of sin. And Protestant Christians are often heard singing a popular hymn in which they say "Jesus paid it all, all to him I owe. . . ." That is to say, Christians continue to make the claim that mankind owes something to God. And the significance of Jesus is that he managed to pay the debt owed to God.

Index

Index